EVOLUTIONARY CREATIONISM
KABBALA SOLVES THE RIDDLE OF MISSING LINKS

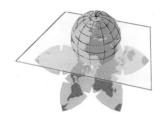

SARAH YEHUDIT SCHNEIDER

✳ *Published with the holy help of* ✳
The Rothkoph Family, The Shlossman Family
and Chana Gross

Friends of

A STILL SMALL VOICE
Correspondence Teachings in Classic Jewish Wisdom
Jerusalem

Published by:

A Still Small Voice
P.O.B 14503
Jerusalem 91141
ISRAEL

TEL: (02) 628-2988
FAX: (02) 628-8302

EMAIL: smlvoice@netvision.net.il
WEBSITE: www.amyisrael.co.il/smallvoice/

בס״ד

The publication of this book
was made possible, through a gift
by the Rothkoph family in memory of,

Yehuda Leib ben Moshe Mordecai
and **Sarah bas Eliezer**

יהודה ליב בן משה מרדכי ושרה בת אליעזר

of blessed memory,

May their souls be bound in the bond of
Eternal Life with HaShem.
תהא נשמתיהם צרורה בצרור החיים

"To those who don't believe, there are no
answers. To those who do believe, there are
no questions."
(Rav Chayim M'Velozhyn)

הרב לוי יצחק הלוי הורוויץ

בס״ד

דער באסטאנער רבי

Grand Rabbi Levi Y. Horowitz

"I feel that this endeavor is very worthwhile. Even the person with greater background will find new thoughts to contemplate and study in this work through the author's focus on how to use the practices of Torah, prayer, and mitzvot to enhance one's relationship with Hashem."

Rabbi Levi Y. Horowitz (The Bostoner Rebbe)

Aish HaTorah
College of Jewish Studies

"I hold Ms. Schneider in very high esteem and can verify that she is highly respected, reliable, and that she approaches her work with an exceptional intellectual motivation which constantly inspires...It is rare to find someone with such depth of knowledge and commitment to bringing back the pride of our heritage."

Rabbi Noah Weinberg, Dean

NEVE·YERUSHALAYIM

"...she enables the serious student to taste the vibrant spirituality of Judaism that permeates even its most basic principles of faith and practice through her creative treatment of the subject, and emphasis on internalizing the information... I warmly recommend A Still Small Voice to anyone who is interested in enriching their lives with the spiritual content of Judaism."

Rabbi David Refson, Rosh Yeshiva

THE HERITAGE בית HOUSE המסורה

RABBI MEIR SCHUSTER
FOUNDER & DIRECTOR

RABBI AVRAHAM EDELSTON
EXECUTIVE DIRECTOR

"Of all our staff in the women's hostel over the years, Susie has stood out as the person most capable of answering the wide range of questions that have come up. She has worked hard both to acquire the necessary knowledge and to find ways of translating this into the language of the unaffiliated."

Rabbi Meir Schuster

כפר חב״ד, טל׳ — 9607-351-03
מגדל־עדר, גוש־עציון, ד.נ. צפון יהודה
טל׳ 204־932־02

"I have been impressed by Susan Schneider's knowledge of Torah in general and Chassidut in particular, as well as her command of the English language and ability to deftly convey even very abstract ideas clearly... I trust her ability to develop and elaborate raw ideas into cogent, well-researched expositions."

Rabbi Yitzchak Ginsburgh

Network of ☺ CONSCIOUS JUDAISM

"This course draws on mysticism and mainstream Judaism, and covers a wide range of essential issues and practices. It is not pushy, but it demands time, and thought and commitment... You will be challenged and stimulated... It is very provoking for the beginner and advanced alike."

Rabbi David Zeller

Gal Einai

ג	ל	ע	י	נ	י
ו	א	כ	י	ט	ה
נ	פ	ל	א	ו	ת
מ	ה	י	ר	ה	ל

גַּל־עֵינַי

ת.ד. 545, רחובות 76100, טל: 936-5947 (08); פקס: 947-3843 (08)
P.O. Box 545, Rechovot 76100, Israel; tel: +972-8-936-5947; fax: +972-8-947-3043
E-mail: inner@inner.org   Web page: http://www.inner.org

בס"ד
י"ת שבט היתש"ס

To whom it may concern:

I have known Sarah Yehudit (Susan) Schneider of Jerusalem for approximately eighteen years. During this time I have been positively impressed by her knowledge of Torah in general and *Chassidut* in particular, as well as her command of the English language and ability to articulate even very abstract ideas clearly and succinctly. In additjion, I trust her ability to develop and elaborate concepts into cogent, well-researched exposition. She has written several articles and a book for Gal Einai, and I was very satisfied with her work each time.

I am confident that her present work reflects her established scholarly reputation.

Sincerely,

Yitzchak Ginsburgh

Yitzchak Ginsburgh

YG:mw

TABLE OF CONTENTS

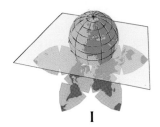

I
EVOLUTIONARY CREATIONISM
Kabbala[1] Solves the Riddle of Missing Links

The popular debate between evolutionists and creationists has nothing to do with Torah,[2] for both champion opinions that conflict with Torah's timeless truths. Yet there is reality to each position as well, and the expansive vision of Kabbala identifies those truths and reconciles them. The result is paradigm shift and a glimpse into higher worlds.

---

[1] Kabbala – Literally, the received tradition, or the science of correspondences. That part of the oral tradition which presents the inner and mystical interpretations of the Torah and its practices.

[2] See Glossary for a full definition of this word.

The zealots of evolution assert that once science discovers the mechanics of a natural process it *proves* the non existence of God in that realm.[3] This atheistic approach to science is succinctly expressed by Yuri Gagarin, the Russian cosmonaut. Hurling through the heavens, he peers out his porthole and briefs his comrades at ground control, "I don't see God, God does not exist." His assumption is that, wherever a natural explanation exists, God does not. He postulates a mutually exclusive relationship between science and religion.[4] Jewish theology asserts the opposite, and practicing Jews affirm that principle in their six-word statement of faith (called the *Shema*) which proclaims the absolute oneness of God.[5]

---

[3] A simple, working definition of God: The essential name of God in Judaism is built from all the permutations of the verb, "to be." It thus translates as, *that which was, is, and will always be.*

[4] Pure science is agnostic; it neither asserts nor refutes the notion of God. Proof is the wide range of opinions that scientists hold on this matter. See: Ken Wilber, ed., *Quantum Questions, Mystical Writings of the World's Great Physicists*, (Boston, MA: Shambhala Press, 1985).

[5] Deut. 6:4. "Hear [Know] Israel, God our Lord, God is one." (*Shema Yisrael Adon-oi E-lohaynu Adon-oi ach*ed.) The name *Adon-oi* is actually a name that we substitute

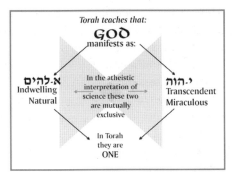

The *Shema* includes two names of God (*Adon-oi*[5] and *E-lohim*), which express two different modes of Divine interaction with creation. *Adon-oi*[5] indicates the transcendent aspect of Divinity (י-הוה) that exists beyond time and space, beyond name and form. Conversely, *E-lohim* is the name used throughout the creation chapters of Genesis. It refers to the indwelling aspect of God that operates in the world and within the constraints of natural law. The *Shema* declares that *miracle* and *nature* are simply two modes of Divine expression. There is nothing but God. All of physical reality is nothing but

---

when encountering the four-letter, unutterable name of God in the text of prayer or study. That four-letter name appears in the diagram above.

Divinity in a state of concealment and contraction. *Un*concealed and *un*contracted God manifests as Infinite Light. Concealed and contracted God manifests as the physical world.

Torah teaches, through the *Shema* as its central article of faith, that the same God that dwells above nature (and can override it at will) is also the force that acts through the laws of nature for these are equally expressions of Divine will. *Adon-oi*[5](יהוה-י) and *E-lohim* are one.

From this perspective, evolution and genesis need not conflict. It is possible that Divinity brought forth the effulgence of life through a process that resembled evolution. There are authoritative commentaries that arrive at similar conclusions.[6] Yet still, the question remains, "Even if the Darwinian model of evolution *could* be true, is it really the best explanation of the facts at hand?" That is the question explored herein, and it leads to surprising and exciting solutions.

On the other side of the debate is the particular interpretation of genesis, called

---

[6] For a sampling of these commentaries see: Susan Schneider, "*Evolution—Form and Consciousness*," *B'Or HaTorah*, Number 4, 1984, pp. 14-38.

creationism, which also bears little, if any, resemblance to Jewish thought. It is a basic principle of Torah that every verse in the Bible has four levels of interpretation, an acronym for which is the four-letter word PaRDeS (Hebrew for "garden," and root of the English word "paradise").

1) "P" (*Pshat*) is its literal meaning and narrative intent; the plot or story line.

2) "R" (*Remez*) is the level of hint whereby peculiarities of grammar, spelling, and syntax hint to deeper levels of interrelationship within the text.

3) "D" (*Drash* also called *Midrash*) is the homiletical level of interpretation where the entire Bible is understood as a metaphor for each individual soul's unfolding. Everyone has an aspect of Abraham that must be willing to sacrifice Isaac, every one must receive the Torah at Sinai, etc.

4) "S" (*Sod*) is the secret, mystical or kabbalistic level of interpretation that hints to the inner worlds, angelic kingdoms and mathematical intricacies of Divinity.

Creationism only incorporates the first, or literal level of meaning, into its theology. And beyond PaRDeS, which applies to every passage in the Bible, Kabbala has focused intently upon the first chapters of Genesis for it is known that they conceal the deepest secrets of the universe. Volumes of mystical commentary abound. An entire book, called *Tikunei Zohar,* is written on the first word alone.

Thus creationism, though it cites the Bible as its source, is a non-Jewish phenomenon, since it does not incorporate the full range of Torah commentaries on the subject.

This paper presents a kabbalistic perspective on Genesis, built from traditional sources, and proposes an exciting framework for integrating those ancient teachings with the cutting edge of scientific research on the origin of our universe.

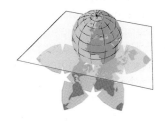

DYNAMIC PARADOX: A METHODOLOGY OF RECONCILIATION

The methodology employed here is called Dynamic Paradox. It is premised on the certainty that the facts of nature can never contradict the truths of Torah.[7] Jewish tradition teaches that the ten statements of "Let there be…", cited in Genesis, are the means by which Divinity brought forth the entirety of creation.[8]

---

[7] This is one interpretation of the religious prohibition against "believing in any power other than God." See: Sarah Yehudit Schneider, *A Still Small Voice*, Correspondence Teachings in Jewish Wisdom. *Synchrony*, Lesson 9.

[8] Actually the phrase, "Let there be…" only appears nine times. The Talmud then counts the first verse of Genesis, "In the beginning…" as the tenth fiat (TB Megila 21b).

And these ten statements correspond, one to one, with the Ten Commandments, which contain the entire fabric of Jewish theology. God expresses Himself through each, though in the first He employs the language of symbol (i.e. the objects of creation and natural law), while in the latter He uses words and sentences.[9] Yet each, in its own alphabet, presents the full content of Divinity's communication with creation. There can be no contradiction between them, for both derive from the same *One* that conceived creation, birthed it into being, and then revealed *His* will for that creation at Sinai.

---

[9] God is beyond gender, containing both male and female elements as well as levels of oneness where even the duality of gender does not exist. The essential name of God, called the Tetragramaton, is androgynous. It contains two masculine letters (ו ,י) and two feminine letters (ה ,ה). Similarly, Genesis 1:27 describes the first human as "created in the image of G-d...male and female." Nevertheless the dilemma remains of which gendered pronoun to use when writing about G-d. The author has chosen to continue with the custom of "He" simply because changing this implies various ideological affiliations and associations that are not hers.

Any discrepancy between the empirical "facts" of nature and the theological "facts" of Torah is only apparent, and resolution must be sought. The approach to resolving any conflict is twofold:

First, one examines the evidence of science to assess its reliability. What is fact and what is theory? What underlying assumptions might distort its interpretation of the data? What is the deeper significance of its findings?

Second, one looks within the vast body of material that comprises the traditional teachings of Torah to search for evidence that supports the facts (or assertions) of science. Are there statements in the Bible, Talmud, *Midrash*,[10] Kabbala, (i.e. in the PaRDeS), which present compatible ideas or suggest equivalent frameworks? Back and forth, from science to Torah and back again, one hammers out a synthesis that fuses the unique insights of both worlds.

---

[10] See glossary.

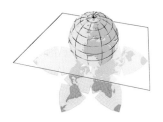

SYNCHRONIZING OUR WATCHES

Step one is to clarify exactly how these two visions of creation (science and Torah) line up in time. What interval in the timeline of history is each attempting to expound? Is evolution explaining the same sequence of events recounted in the Torah's seven creation days?

That is what people generally assume. However, a careful look at the teachings suggests a different and quite startling conclusion.

The place to begin is with the largest frame of both science and Torah, and to see how these two scenarios line up on a macro scale. Beginning with science, what is its most current theory concerning the origin of our universe? Then, turning to Torah and drawing from commentaries on all levels of PaRDeS, what does it say about the sequence of events and the nature of reality in the first seven days of creation? Sparks fly from the dialogue between them, and a synthesis emerges—a paradigm shift—that incorporates the highest truths of both worlds.

A Scientific History of Creation

Breakthroughs in particle physics, mathematics and cosmology have revolutionized our understanding of the natural world. Brian Green, an eminent Harvard physicist who wrote a wonderfully informative book called the *Elegant Universe*, speaks as follows:

> For the first time in the history of physics we have a framework with the capacity to explain every fundamental feature upon which the universe is constructed... This theory is called Superstrings, and a series of astonishing breakthroughs in physics within the last two decades have culminated in its development, indicating that perhaps we are finally closing in on the unified field theory: a comprehensive,

mathematical framework that would unite all the known forces of the universe.[11]

The term Superstrings (or string theory) comes from the realization that our fundamental particles (quarks and electrons) are not really particles at all, but tiny loops.

> Everything, at its most microscopic level, consists of vibrating, filaments called strings…Just as the strings on a violin resonate at frequencies that our ears recognize as musical notes, the same holds true for the loops of string theory. But rather than producing musical notes…each pattern of vibration appears as a particle whose mass and features are determined by the strings' vibratory pattern.[12]

This slight adjustment in our understanding of the fundamental constituents of matter – that they are strings instead of points – has revolutionized modern physics in welcomed and not-so-welcomed ways. On the one hand Superstrings is stunning in its ability to resolve most of the major problems of 20th century physics: It reconciles Einstein's relativity with Quantum Mechanics; it predicts the pattern and

---

[11] Brian Greene, *The Elegant Universe* (Vintage Books, 1999) p. 16 (18).

[12] Greene, p. 15.

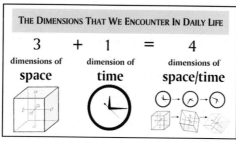

THE DIMENSIONS THAT WE ENCOUNTER IN DAILY LIFE

3	+	1	=	4
dimensions of **space**		dimension of **time**		dimensions of **space/time**

properties of our fundamental particles; it integrates all four fundamental forces. On the other hand, all this only happens if one posits that there are actually 9+1[13] spatial dimensions in our universe plus time which totals eleven (i.e., 10+1).

This is a less welcomed feature for it not only grates against our common sense experience of the world; it contradicts all of our patiently acquired empirical evidence from time immemorial. As long as we have studied the universe, even with all our high-powered

---

[13] It is written 9+1 and 10+1 because the *+1* dimension was more recently discovered, and it functions as a kind of integrator. This accords precisely with Kabbalistic map of the world called the Tree of Life with its 10+1 *sefirot* where the meta-*sephira*, called *daat*, functions as the (*+1*) integrator, for the *Sefer Yetzira* declares, there are "ten and not eleven" *sefirot*.

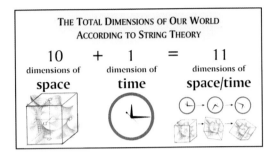

THE TOTAL DIMENSIONS OF OUR WORLD
ACCORDING TO STRING THEORY

10 + 1 = 11

dimensions of   dimension of   dimensions of

space   **time**   **space/time**

detectors, we have only encountered four dimensions, three of space and one of time. And these have been perfectly sufficient to explain our experience.

Nevertheless, string theory teaches, as an intrinsic part of its model, that our universe has ten spatial dimensions, though only the familiar three of length, breadth and height, seem to be active and manifest today. The other seven collapsed, according to scientists, at some early point in cosmic history.[14] Quoting from Michio

---

[14] Kaku and Trainer (see footnote 15) describe the sequence: 1) ten unfurled spatial dimensions that then ruptured, 2) seven dimensions collapse and three remain manifest; 3) this triggers an inflationary process that results in the Big Bang. Greene also presents this scenario (p. 361-363), as well as an alternate perspective (p. 204). In his alternative scenario, history

Kaku and Jennifer Trainer's book, *Beyond Einstein*[15,16]:

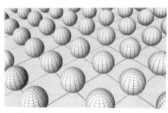

Like a dam bursting, the ten dimensional fabric of space-time ruptured violently and rapidly reformed into two [yoked and bound] universes of lower energy: a four dimensional

Each globe represents a knot of seven dimensions collapsed into a submolecular black hole that lies within and behind each point of our familiar physical world represented by the grid that extends in all directions.

universe (our own) and a six dimensional one [collapsed into an infinite array of

---

began with all ten dimensions collapsed down into a tight knot. Then, with the Big Bang, three dimensions unfurled and seven remained collapsed. In the parallel sequence of events presented by Kabbala, these two scenarios could each represent different intervals in the long sequence of pre-Edenic history. (See footnote 22).

[15] Dr. Michio Kaku and Jennifer Trainer, *Beyond Einstein: The Cosmic Quest for the Theory of the Universe* (Bantam New Age Books, 1987) p. 158.

[16] Image from: http://people.cs.uchicago.edu/~mbw/astro18200/sphere grid-small.jpg.

submicroscopic knots, within and behind it]...In this picture, the Big Bang and our expanding universe are, in some sense, nothing but the debris left over from a titanic rupture in the structure of space-time itself.

The obvious question arises: What does it mean to live in a ten dimensional world? What do these other dimensions look like now? What *would* they look like if they were unfurled, instead of collapsed down into nearly invisible knots? Scientists explain that it is impossible for us to imagine a ten-dimensional object (let alone a universe). We would not even be able to see one if it were right before our eyes. Our visual cortex can only process three dimensions at a time.

> Our minds, which conceptualize objects in three spatial dimensions, cannot fully grasp higher dimensional objects. Even physicists and mathematicians, who regularly handle higher-dimensional objects in their research, treat these objects with abstract mathematics rather than trying to visualize them.[17]

The physical features of this primordial universe defy description. Our language is confined by the four-dimensional consciousness

---

[17] Kaku and Trainer, p. 166.

that spawned it. The mathematics of modern physics posit the *fact* of a multi-dimensional world that preceded our own, but cannot paint its picture for our mind's eye.

To summarize: according to Superstrings, our universe originally existed in ten spatial dimensions, and that period is impossible for us to imagine. At some point it shattered, collapsed, and reformed into our familiar reality of three, yet those extra seven dimensions are still present but hidden. A fully unfurled ten-dimensional universe preceded the big bang, while our familiar three-dimensional world followed it.

The scientific quest called cosmology has, until now, been limited to the three dimensional reality that comprises our familiar, post Big Bang world. Yet with the discovery of superstrings, the periscope of science has begun to peep around the corner and glimpse some features of a multi-dimensional universe that likely preceded our own three-dimensional world.

A Brief History of the Universe According To the Insights of Torah

Interestingly, the *midrashic*[18] descriptions of Eden and *Adam*'s "fall" present a scenario of crash and repair that is nearly identical to the account of prehistory derived from superstrings.[19] Yet Torah also struggles with the limitations of language when it tries to depict the scintillating features of Gan Eden (the Garden of Eden). Its *midrashim* tackle the dilemma by invoking poetic license to weave fantasy and metaphor into a story-like account of the early universe offering a traditional interpretation which accords precisely with the scenario proposed by theoretical physicists. Their resemblance is truly striking.

Judaism teaches that every story in the Torah is always literally true. In addition to the psychological and metaphysical teachings which are also present, the Bible's stories are actual historical occurrences. Kabbala explains, however, that although the first chapters of

---

[18] *See* Glossary for a definition of this term.

[19] The original human being was created as a single body combining both male and female aspects who were, together, called *Adam*.

Genesis *did* literally happen *and* are real events, they transpired on an entirely different plane of reality than what we experience as the physical world today.[20] Until Adam and Eve ate from the Tree of Knowledge of Good and Evil, the lowest level of the universe was the mental plane (which Kabbala calls the World of Creation, in Hebrew *Briyah*). This means that the bodies and objects of that era were actually more like thought forms.

When Adam and Eve ate from the Tree of Knowledge they caused an intermingling of good and evil for the first time in history and reality transformed completely. It turned inside out, upside down, and tumbled level after level before collapsing into the configuration that we now experience as the physical plane.[21]

Rabbi Shlomo Elyashiv, a master kabbalist of the late 19th century known as the *Leshem*, describes this catastrophic event as follows: [22]

---

[20] Zohar III, *Kedoshim* 83a; R. S. Elyashev, *HaDrush Olam Hatohu*, II, p. 16, 79.

[21] Zohar III, *Kedoshim* 83a.

[22] According to Kabbala, a shattering occurred at each stage in the unfolding of reality from its inception in the mind of God to its materialization as a physical fact.

When *Adam*[23] ate from the Tree of Knowledge his Edenic world fell level after level, its light thickening and thickening until it acquired the opaque material properties of our physical plane...Though, most of the original permeating light withdrew back up to its root...some of its sparks got trapped in the thickening light and fell too, collapsing into dense seed-like points of dark light the size of grasshopper antennas

---

Creation did not unfold smoothly, but rather alternated between shattering and repair, shattering and repair. In this composited quotation above, some of the descriptions refer to an earlier shattering, before Adam and Eve and their Garden had yet appeared on the scene. Nevertheless, these same passages continue with the following words: "While most of this original shattering was reversed and repaired during the six days of creation, when Adam and Eve ate from the Tree of Knowledge they completely undid that repair." This primordial shattering was thus reenacted by *Adam*. Creation reverted to the splintered, fallen state described herein.

[23] *Adam* is not male. Rather the Biblical term *Adam* includes Adam and Eve. The Torah initially describes the creation of the first human being as follows (Gen. 1:27): "And God created Adam in His own image. In the image of God He created him, male and female He created them." Jewish tradition teaches that the original human being was created as a single body combining both male and female aspects.

(קרני חגבים). These are called *gevurot*, and they are strewn throughout the fabric of creation.[24]

This kabbalistic description of Eden's fall echoes the scientific tale of ruptured space-time called the Big Bang. And, as we shall see, Kabbala goes even beyond science in its capacity to provide certain details concerning that mysterious era of cosmic history, before the Big Bang (BBB). Science does not yet have the instruments to probe behind that cataclysmic event. All it can say now is that BBB reality had ten special dimensions. Kabbala concurs and elaborates. [25]

The Torah's symbolic language and story-like approach might seem strange to scientists who are used to a more linear presentation of

---

[24] לשם שבו ואחלמה, הדעי״ת, הדרש עץ הדעת, סימן י״ד, ד״ה (ונחזר); I 5 rt col toward bottom, also left column, very bottom; p 294 rt col; ספר הקדוי״ש שער ו׳ פרקים י׳ וי״א. All of these citations appear in full in Appendix 4.

[25] The kabbalistic teachings cited in this essay are less than a drop in the vast sea of kabbalistic writings on prehistory. Rabbi Elyashev (the *Leshem*), wrote a book called, *Essay on the Worlds of Chaos*, that concerns the various eras of history before the Torah begins its creation story.

information. Nevertheless, its conclusions about the nature of cosmic prehistory are nearly identical to those of modern physics. The Torah employs symbols where science employs math. Unfortunately, many of its symbols are burdened with centuries of misuse. Their popular associations often bear little resemblance to their actual meaning within a Torah frame. For example, in order to proceed we must present a working definition of *evil,* since the Torah's tale revolves around the Tree of Knowledge of Good and *Evil* and evil plays a major role in the *Big Bang* as narrated by Kabbala.

What does that term really mean? Evil, in Judaism, is the illusion of separation and independence from God. The word "illusion" is significant. Nothing can actually be separate from Divinity because God is one. To the extent that something presents the appearance of self-containment, self-sovereignty, and multiplicity, to that extent it partakes of the quality of evil. To the extent that it communicates through itself the truth of God's existence, goodness, oneness, compassion, and generosity, to that extent it partakes of the quality of holiness.

Before the catastrophic event called the *fall*, both good and evil existed in Eden, but each as a sphere unto itself. [26] The territory of holiness and the territory of concealment did not intermix, except in one small area of overlap, called the Tree of Knowledge of Good and Evil. Since the fall, truth and illusion are always entwined. There is no good without evil and no evil without good. This was not so in Eden. Adam and Eve were absolutely pure, enlightened beings, immaculate through and through. Their only impulse was to serve God, and there was not the slightest taint to their souls. Evil (i.e., concealment) existed in Eden but as a creature unto itself, embodied as the infamous serpent wrapped around the Tree of Knowledge, and functioning as its *voice*. [27]

---

[26] Most of the ideas in this section come from Rabbi Eliyahu Dessler's discussion of the subject in: *Michtav M'Eliyahu*, Vol. II, pp. 135-145.

[27] For an explanation of how they could choose to violate God's command and eat from the Tree of Knowledge if they were so pure and enlightened, see Rav Eliyahu Dessler, *Michtav Me'Eliyahu*, Vol 2, p. 137-145.

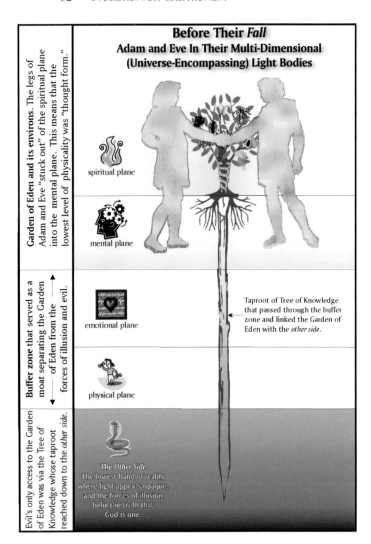

Before Their *Fall*
Adam and Eve In Their Multi-Dimensional
(Universe-Encompassing) Light Bodies

Garden of Eden and its environs. The legs of Adam and Eve "stuck out" of the spiritual plane into the mental plane. This means that the lowest level of physicality was "thought form."

spiritual plane

mental plane

Buffer zone that served as a moat separating the Garden of Eden from the forces of illusion and evil.

emotional plane

physical plane

Taproot of Tree of Knowledge that passed through the buffer zone and linked the Garden of Eden with the *other side*.

Evil's only access to the Garden of Eden was via the Tree of Knowledge whose taproot reached down to the *other side*.

The *Other Side*
The lowest band of reality where light appears opaque, and the forces of illusion belie the truth that God is one.

		After The Fall
		Adam and Eve (Humanity) In Their Fallen,
		Darkened, And Shattered State

Spiritual Plane remains untouched by the forces of illusion (evil), yet its level of consciousness is virtually inaccessible to us who are now below.

spiritual plane

The forces of illusion (and darkness) now extend through the emotional and mental planes, clouding vision and distorting awareness.

mental plane

emotional plane

Adam and Eve shattered into a near infinity of sparks that comprise the generations of humanity till the end of time.

The area of overlap between the physical plane and the *other side* is the metaphysical niche currently occupied by humankind.

physical plane

The *Other Side*
The lowest band of reality
where light appears opaque,
and the forces of illusion
belie the truth that
God is one.

For Adam and Eve, to *eat* from the Tree of Knowledge meant bringing its mixture of good and evil *into* themselves. *Eating* is the archetype of taking something from the outside and bringing it in so that it loses its own identity and becomes part of the consumer. When they imbibed the "*knowledge* of good and evil," Adam and Eve absorbed its cloudy consciousness into the cells and substance of their being. The illusion of other-than-God spread through their systems and entered all the places where clarity had previously dwelled. Their God-consciousness collapsed into self-consciousness. The entire world was affected, and from that moment on, every truth contained at least a trace of distortion, and every lie at least a trace of fact.

Evil expresses itself differently on each plane, whether physical, emotional, mental, or spiritual. The manifestation of evil (or separation from God) in physical substance is the fact of its boundedness. Matter has outline. Physical objects have skins or shells which delineate them as separate entities. A book is distinct from the table, which is distinct from the chair, which is distinct from the person sitting upon it. Matter presents the appearance of many. The outer eyes report multiplicity with oneness nowhere to be found. Only a penetrating vision can tunnel through appearances and behold the pattern of unity that hides beneath. This feature of our physical world was not always so. Rather it is a product of *Adam*'s eating from the Tree of Knowledge and the subsequent intermingling of good and evil that ensued. In this sense our world bears no resemblance to the physical reality of Eden and the seven days of Genesis.

Though both pre and post Edenic realities are physical, the term means something different in each context. *Now* matter is "bounded," *then* it was not. In trying to imagine what this means one hits the same obstacle that physicists meet when attempting to depict the ten dimensional world proposed by modern science as the starting point of our universe. *Unbounded matter* is Torah's way of signifying this same higher dimensional state. These two narratives (centuries apart) are equivalent in this regard, and to visualize either multi dimensions or unbounded matter is simply not possible (at least at this point in the unfolding of consciousness).[28]

The *midrash* attempts to circumvent this problem by asking its readers to stretch beyond their habitual mind set and accept two "impossible" facts about Edenic *Adam*:

- his body was light, and

- he contained the universe within himself.

To elaborate:

His body was light.

After Adam and Eve ate from the forbidden Tree of Knowledge, and faced the devastating consequences of their deed, the Bible recounts a further encounter between themselves and their Creator.

> And the Lord God made for the man and his wife *garments of skin* and clothed them. [29]

The words for *skin* and *light* are homonyms in Hebrew.[30] They sound alike but are spelled

---

[28] Even light is "bounded" to the extent that (from one perspective) it is comprised of finite packets of energy called, quanta.

[29] Genesis 3:21.

[30] Or nearly so. In fact, when properly pronounced, the ע is more guttural than the א.

differently. עור ('*or*) with an ע means skin and אור (*or*) with an א means light.

Based on this relationship, the 2nd century teacher, Rabbi Meir explains that these "garments of skin" are not just leather tunics, like clothing today. Rather the verse is teaching us that now, for the first time, Divinity enclothed their souls in an opaque, leathery skin, i.e. a physical body. Quoting Rabbi Meir, the Talmud states:

> Originally *Adam's* body was made of light (אוֹר) [*or*]. But after he sinned God clothed his body in [a thick, opaque covering called] skin (עוֹר) ['*or*].[31]

Thus, according to R. Meir, the Torah itself is teaching that originally Adam and Eve had radiant bodies of light. Only after their sin did they acquire physical bodies as we experience them now.

Another *midrash* is equally explicit in depicting *Adam* as a radiant body of light:

> The heels of *Adam*'s dead body were like two radiant suns."[32] If his heels shone thus, imagine

---

[31] *Bereshit Rabba* 20:29.

[32] TB *Baba Batra* 58a.

the light of his head...and even more before his death... and even more, before he sinned.[33]

These *midrashim* written approximately 1700 years before modern physics, thus teach that Adam and Eve were glowing bodies of light.

It is more accurate to imagine the physicality of Eden as translucent, shimmering, and unbounded, a condition that differs completely from the opaque and limited physicality we experience today.

The second other-worldly feature of *Adam*, according to the *midrash*, is that:

He contained the universe within himself.

The Talmud states:

The first human being spanned from the heavens to the earth, and from one end of the world to its other end.[34]

Our sages teach thereby that *Adam* contained the universe *within* himself. Not like now where humans are little creatures moving within a huge cosmos. Rather *Adam* was a

---

[33] Raabbi Eliyahu Dessler, *Michtav M'Eliyahu*, Vol. II, pp. 135-145.

[34] TB *Chagiga 12a.*

single, all-inclusive entity. The other creatures
and kingdoms in Eden were layers and organs
within his universe-encompassing "body." *Adam
was* the whole universe. [35]

> So awesome and god-like was this *Adam* that
> the angels actually erred and began to serve
> him as though he were God.[36]

All this was lost when Adam and Eve ate
from the Tree of Knowledge of Good and Evil,
and the universe turned inside out, upside
down and crashed into its current four-
dimensional form. The *midrash* explains that
one consequence of their act was a drastic
shrinking of stature. It derives its interpretation
from the verse describing Adam and Eve's
embarrassed attempt to avoid the frightful
consequences of their deed. The verse reads:

> And they heard the voice of God moving
> through the garden. The man and his wife hid
> themselves from God among the trees of the
> garden. [37]

The *midrash* highlights the obvious implications
of this verse.

---

[35] *Michtav M'Eliyahu*, Vol. II, pp. 135-145.

[36] *Bereshit Rabba 8.*

[37] *Genesis 3:10,*

God rebuked *Adam*: *"Yesterday* you spanned from one end of the world to the other; now, You [can] hide yourselves among the trees."

The fact that *Adam* could hide behind a tree was tell-tale proof of his deed. Yesterday (before his sin) *Adam* contained the "trees" (and all of reality) within himself. Now, in his newly fallen state, he is one creature among many, and not even the most majestic of them. Now, a simple tree towers above him.

These *midrashim* depict a universe drastically different from ours where *Adam* was a light-being who contained the entire universe inside himself. Their point is to distinguish Eden from our fallen, shattered, darkened reality. We cannot extrapolate from here to there. Unlike our world with its myriad of disconnected creatures, Eden was different. The lowest, densest layer of physicality was light-like and the entirety of creation was a single coordinated, living entity called *Adam*.

The Timeline of Evolutionary History Overlaid Onto Genesis

This concurrence of Torah and physics regarding the multi-dimensional features of our early universe is stunning. Both posit an initial period of history when physicality was not like our own, and a drastic transitional event that brought forth our world in its present form.

Lining these two theories up, it becomes clear that the Torah's creation days actually precede the Big Bang. Their multi-dimensional reality parallels the period before the cosmic rupture when all ten spatial dimensions were still unfurled. *Adam* was created on the "sixth day," and according to the Talmud, he ate from the Tree of Knowledge in the 10th hour (from sunrise) and was expelled in the 12th hour (i.e., just before sunset).[38] At that point the universe fell, ten dimensions collapsed into three, and *Adam* found himself hiding among the trees. If the *midrashic* collapse of Eden equates with the cosmic rupture that triggered the Big Bang,[39] then the disparity between scientific history and

---

[38] Babylonian Talmud, Sanhedrin 38b. In the Jewish calendar a day begins with sunset. "And there was evening, and there was morning, Day One" (Gen. 1:3).

[39] A footnote for those learned in Hebrew texts: Though God spared Adam and Eve the full consequence of their deed until after Shabbat, nevertheless, they were already "hiding among the trees" on the sixth day, so some measure of collapse had already occurred.

the Biblical timeline becomes even more gaping than is usually assumed. In this corrected model, the billions of years of evolutionary history no longer coincide with the six creation days (as creationists generally assert). Rather they occur within the last hour of the sixth creation day when *Adam*, according to the Talmud, was expelled from Eden. This means that what appears from the perspective of the mental plane (the World of *Briyah*) as a single hour, is experienced by us here below, on the physical plane (the World of *Asiyah*) as billions of years. [40]

---

[40] According to Rabbi Elyashev (the *Leshem*), the first five creation days did happen on the physical plane, but one that was totally different from our physical world today. The physical plane of Genesis was *unbounded*. There were no skins that demarcated one creature from another. This is virtually impossible for us to imagine. Then, with Adam's appearance on the sixth day, all of reality ascended to the mental plane and the events of the sixth day transpired there. Since the focus of *this* discussion is Adam (and Eden) before the fall and after, which, by all accounts, occurred on the mental plane (*Briyah*) the graph on the following page simplifies these details and depicts all six creation days as occurring there, for all agree that reality was in *briyah* and above on the on the sixth day.

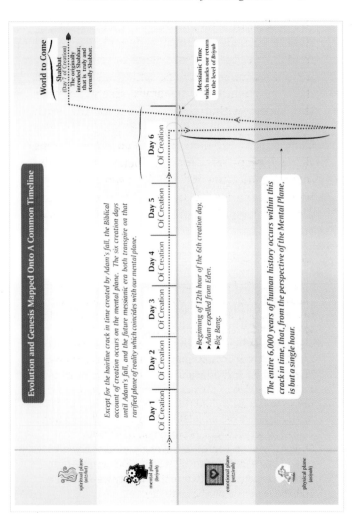

Evolution and Genesis Mapped Onto A Common Timeline

Except for the hairline crack in time created by Adam's fall, the Biblical account of creation occurs on the mental plane. The six creation days until Adam's fall, and the future messianic era both transpire on that rarified plane of reality which coincides with our mental plane.

spiritual plane
(atzilut)

mental plane
(briyah)

emotional plane
(yetzirah)

physical plane
(asiyah)

Day 1
Of Creation

Day 2
Of Creation

Day 3
Of Creation

Day 4
Of Creation

Day 5
Of Creation

Day 6
Of Creation

World to Come

Shabbat
(Day 7 of Creation)
The originally
intended Shabbat,
that is truly and
eternally Shabbat.

Messianic Time
which marks our return
to the level of Briyah

► Beginning of 12th hour of the 6th creation day.
► Adam expelled from Eden.
► Big Bang.

The entire 6,000 years of human history occurs within this crack in time, that, from the perspective of the Mental Plane, is but a single hour.

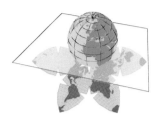

EVOLUTIONARY THEORY – FACT AND THEORY

What happened when Eden collapsed after the fall? How did *Adam*'s universe-encompassing body reconstitute itself on the physical plane? Did it proceed though an evolutionary-like process as Darwin proposed? The Torah does not provide details of how this transition from the unity of the mental plane to the multiplicity of the physical plane occurred. Any number of scenarios are consistent with Genesis, including Darwin's evolutionary model.[41]

---

[41] For a cogent, source-based explication of how this could be so, see: Susan Schneider, "Evolution—form and Consciousness," *B'Or HaTorah, Number 4, 1984, pp. 14-38.*

It is clear that one of the primary appeals of evolutionary theory is that it mirrors our own experience of change. Many are loyal to Darwin's model simply because of their deep identification with its paradigm. In the human experience, change and evolution are nearly synonymous. In every realm—culture, technology, physiology, psychology—growth imitates the evolutionary model. Sometimes graduated, sometimes punctuated, the universe moves persistently and progressively forward— stage by stage, each stage emerging out of the last—toward increasing sophistication and perfection. Wherever we look we see evolution at work. And yet, the fact remains, that the fossil record of our planet does not support the neo-Darwinian model. Some scientists are calling for an honest and dispassionate review of the evidence (or lack thereof). In their ground-breaking work, called, *The New Biology*, Robert Augros and George Stanciu voice a growing trend among biologists who are questioning Darwin's model of competitive survival and moving toward a new theory of cooperation and harmony in nature:

> How could natural selection be controversial? It seems so cogent and plausible. One of its appeals has always been its intrinsic logic.

However, its critics do not question Darwin's logic but the verifiable truth of his premises. All of his key assumptions...conflict with the results of modern ecological studies and genetic research...The way nature acts right now does not agree with Darwin's premises.

Evolutionary theory today, like physics in the nineteenth century stands at a crossroad...The most scientific response is to admit the crisis and make a fresh beginning, to examine all the evidence without partisanship, and to determine what is known about the history of life, with the realization that this may require us to modify or abandon some of the conventional assumptions of neo-Darwinism. Not only is this alternative reasonable in itself, it also agrees with the whole spirit of Darwin's own work: "I have steadily endeavored to keep my mind free, so as to give up any hypothesis, however much beloved, as soon as facts are shown to be opposed to it."

We must begin again, then, by going back to first principles, carefully separating the known from the unknown, the certain from the doubtful, and the more probable from the less probable. [42]

---

[42] Robert Augros and George Stanciu, *The New Biology, Discovering the Wisdom in Nature* (New Science Library, Shambhala, 1988) p. 158-165. (Emphasis mine).

Taking this advice to heart and going back to first principles, the first distinction to make is between micro evolution, and macro evolution:

Micro evolution describes the process by which members of a species adapt to a changing environment utilizing the mechanisms of random mutation, natural selection and survival of the fittest. In this way, individuals develop variations in appearance and perhaps even evolve into reproductively isolated groups. Micro evolution is tried and true. The evidence for Darwin's theory of micro evolution was and is compelling.

Macro evolution extrapolates from these micro principles and asserts that the present diversity of plant and animal life arose from the earliest and most primitive single-celled organisms through a similar mechanism of natural selection, random mutation and survival of the fittest. And here, the evidence is sparse.

Quoting Darwin himself:

> Geological research, though it has added numerous species to existing and extinct genera, and has made the intervals between some few groups less wide than they otherwise would have been, yet it has done scarcely anything in breaking the distinction between species, by connecting them together by

numerous, fine, intermediate varieties; and the fact this has not occurred, is probably the gravest and most obvious of all the many objections which may be urged against my views.[43]

The motive to find an alternative to Darwin's model is not because it raises theological difficulties, but because it lacks scientific rigor. Theoretically, evolution is compatible with the teachings of Torah. It is not, however, compatible with the facts on the ground.

---

[43] Charles Darwin, *Origin of the Species* (Collier Books, New York 1972) p 41.

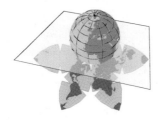

EVOLUTIONARY CREATIONISM – A FUSION OF SCIENCE AND TORAH

Even with all its failings, many find it hard to throw Darwin out. His theory is so elegant. The mind wants it to be true. Scientists are generally cold-blooded empiricists with no patience for suppositions that lack supporting proof. Yet here, they display an uncharacteristic attachment to a theory despite the glaring gap between its predictions and the facts on the ground. There clearly exists an hierarchical progression of complexity in life forms which really does *suggest* a familial relationship between them. Darwin took this suggestion to heart. He speculated that this logical order is actually a history map of evolving complexity. Each higher level emerged literally and gradually from the level before. That is one possible explanation. Yet Kabbala suggests an alternative model that fuses the teachings of Torah with the conclusions of string theory. And what is more, it concurs even better with the facts on the ground. As explained,

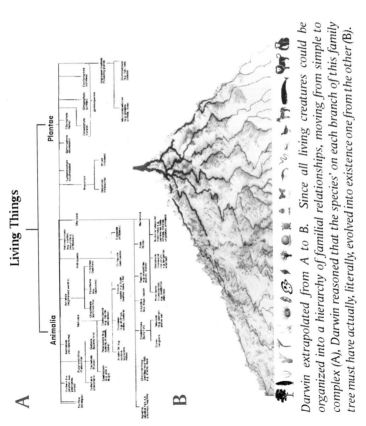

Darwin extrapolated from A to B. Since all living creatures could be organized into a hierarchy of familial relationships, moving from simple to complex (A), Darwin reasoned that the species' on each branch of this family tree must have actually, literally, evolved into existence one from the other (B).

scientists are stumped by the challenge of how to imagine the ten-dimensional reality that they believe exists (as a hidden state even now), and that they believe was the original condition of our BBB reality. The only way they have found to approach the problem is to study lower-dimensional systems and observe what happens when moving from one dimension to the next, i.e. from a point to a line to a plane, to a sphere. Another technique is to imagine what, say, a sphere looks like from the perspective of a plane or a line. The first writer to undertake this task, in the form of a popular novel, was Edwin

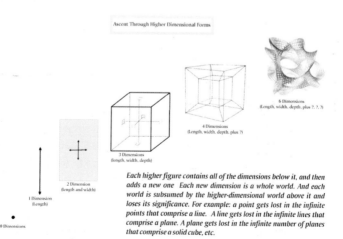

Ascent Through Higher Dimensional Forms

6 Dimensions
(Length, width, depth, plus ?, ?, ?)

4 Dimensions
(Length, width, depth, plus ?)

3 Dimensions
(length, width, depth)

2 Dimension
(length and width)

1 Dimension
(Length)

0 Dimensions

Each higher figure contains all of the dimensions below it, and then adds a new one Each new dimension is a whole world. And each world is subsumed by the higher-dimensional world above it and loses its significance. For example: a point gets lost in the infinite points that comprise a line. A line gets lost in the infinite lines that comprise a plane. A plane gets lost in the infinite number of planes that comprise a solid cube, etc.

A. Abbott, a Shakespearean scholar who in 1884 wrote *Flatland*—a Victorian satire about the curious habits of people who live in two spatial dimensions. Kaku and Trainer summarize the tale and its teachings as follows:

> Imagine the people of Flatland living, say, on the surface of a table. This tale is narrated by the pompous Mr. A. Square, who proudly tells us of a world populated by people who are geometric objects...
>
> Mr. Square, a man of considerable social rank, is content to live in the pampered tranquility of this ordered society, until one day strange beings from Spaceland (a three-dimensional world) appear before Mr. Square and introduce him to the wonders of another dimension.
>
> What happens when higher-dimensional beings enter a lower-dimensional universe? When the mysterious Lord Sphere of Spaceland enters Flatland, Mr. Square can only see circles of ever-increasing size penetrate his universe. Mr. Square cannot visualize Lord Sphere in his entirety, only cross-sections of his shape.
>
> The Lord Sphere even invites Mr. Square to visit Spaceland, which involves a harrowing journey where Mr. Square is peeled off his Flatland world and deposited in the forbidden third dimension. However, as Mr. Square moves

in the third dimension, his eyes can see only two-dimensional cross-sections of three-dimensional Spaceland.

And so is the experience of a Flatlander moving through our universe. As the Flatlander moves in three dimensions and his eyes scan cross-sections, he sees shapes suddenly appear, grow and shrink, change color and then suddenly disappear, defying all the laws of physics of Flatland. For example, think of an ordinary carrot. We can visualize a carrot in its entirety, but a Flatlander cannot. If a carrot is sliced into many circular pieces, a Flatlander can visualize each slice, but never the entire carrot. When the tip of the carrot enters his field of vision, the Flatlander will suddenly see a small orange circle materialize from nowhere. As the Flatlander continues to drift, he will see the orange circle gradually getting bigger.

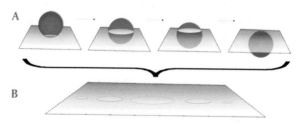

A

B

A. Two-dimensional square (plane) encountering a three dimensional sphere.
B. The two-dimensional plane cannot grasp the totality of the sphere but rather registers a finite series of growing and then diminishing circular cross sections.

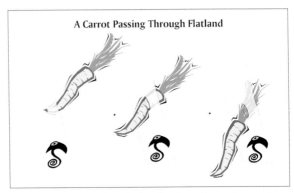

A Carrot Passing Through Flatland

Of course, the Flatlander is only seeing each successive slice of the carrot, which corresponds to circles. Then, the Flatlander sees the orange circle turn into a green circle (which corresponds to the green carrot top). Then suddenly the green circle disappears just as mysteriously as it appeared. *Similarly, if we were to encounter a higher dimensional universe, we would see objects suddenly appear, change color, grow and shrink in size, and then suddenly disappear. Although we might understand that these*

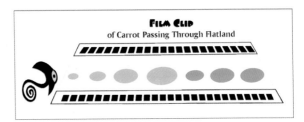

FILM CLIP
of Carrot Passing Through Flatland

various objects were actually part of one higher dimensional object, we would not be able to visualize this object completely, or what life would be like in higher-dimensional space."[44]

This description of a 2-D Flatlander encountering a 3-D world has the makings of a paradigm shift. Its quirky details explain all the paradoxical aspects of Darwinian theory, i.e., most particularly the clear taxonomic relationship between creatures, yet the absence of fossil links connecting them in an evolutionary sequence.

- On the one hand there clearly exists a sequential progression of complexity in life forms, implying a familial relationship between them. The taxonomic tree, as we saw, organizes all creatures, living and extinct, into an orderly series of groups linked by their measure of similarity. This hierarchy of life that connects all organisms together was Darwin's best argument for the gradual evolution of diversity and complexity.

- On the other hand we cannot deny the almost total lack of evidence to support an interconnecting continuum whereby simple

---

[44] Kaku and Trainer, pp. 164-170. Emphasis mine.

forms evolved into more complex ones (whether gradually or by a reasonably punctuated path of biological development). The fossil record does not support Darwin's model in this regard, and current genetic research challenges its feasibility.

Yet, combining the truths of Torah with the models of science, a compelling and intellectually satisfying scenario emerges. The *midrashic* depiction of Eden clearly indicates that it was a multidimensional state. The lowest, densest layer of physicality was light-like and the entirety of creation was a single coordinated, living entity called *Adam*. Unlike our world with its myriad of independent and disconnected creatures moving within it, Eden was different. Not only did, "*Adam* span from the heaven to the earth and from one end of the world to its other," but he (*Adam*) "included within himself the entirety of creation." He *was* the whole universe. All other creatures were simply externalized aspects of his own inner nature. As impossible as it is for a Flatlander to conceive of three-dimensional space, or a scientist to conceptualize a world of ten, *we* cannot imagine the reality of Eden and the first *Adam*.

These ancient teachings regarding Genesis can solve the mystery of evolutionary development. After Adam and Eve ate from the Tree of Knowledge, good and evil became intermingled (as discussed) and Eden reconfigured into the three-dimensional world within which we live today. That singular, and multi-dimensional paradise collapsed into the Flatland of our world. The accounts of Torah and science concur both on the fact of this collapse and the drastic transformations that ensued.

FROM KABBALA

When *Adam* ate from the Tree of Knowledge, his Edenic world shattered… and fell level after level, its light thickening and thickening until it acquired the opaque material properties of our physical plane… Though, most of the original permeating light withdrew back up to its root…some of its sparks got trapped in the thickening light and fell too, collapsing into dense seed-like points of dark light the size of grasshopper antennas (קרני חגבים). These are called *gevurot*, and they are strewn throughout the fabric of creation.

FROM PHYSICS

Like a dam bursting, the ten dimensional fabric of space-time ruptured violently and rapidly reformed into two [yoked and bound] universes of lower energy: a four dimensional universe (our own) and a six dimensional one [collapsed into an infinite array of submicroscopic knots, within and behind it]… In this picture, the Big Bang and our expanding universe are, in some sense, nothing but the debris left over from a titanic rupture in the structure of space-time itself.

And besides the likeness of Kabbala and science in their Big Bang scenarios, the *midrash* adds another similarity when it recounts God's rebuke to Adam and Eve after their misdeed:

> Yesterday you extended from one end of the world to the other; now, "You can hide yourself among the trees of the garden."[45] Yesterday *Adam* contained the "trees" within himself, now they tower above him and he moves beneath and within them.

Taking the story of Flatland and applying it here, yet substituting primordial *Adam* for Lord Sphere, and humanity in its fallen state (i.e., us) for Mr. Square, the story reads as follows:

> When [humanity] encounters the multi-dimensional [*Adam*], the latter appears as a series of discrete and apparently disconnected cross sections. The full extent of the sphere can not squeeze into a two-dimensional visual field. Instead, what registers is a progression of circles, each similar, but not provably connected to the next. They appear one after the other in time, but [humanity's] vision cannot see them all together in one moment, in the same moment, as part of a single, larger whole.

This explains why the taxonomic tree does successfully organize all the species of the world into relatively clear family lines. Now, it makes

---

[45] Genesis 3:

perfect sense. Each cluster of related species must derive from the same limb or organ within that original, universe-encompassing *Adam*. It also explains why, much to Darwin's dismay, the fossil record lacks evidence of transitional forms. What appears as evolution is simply the logical sequence by which ten dimensions transfigure into three. Like a globe transforming into a flattened map. If this is the mechanism, it makes sense that each species would appear discrete and complete.

This is exactly what would be expected if all the *various animal types, in their familial relationships, are actually three-dimensional cross sections of Edenic reality.* This paradigm shift fits all the evidence: we are Flatlanders experiencing

A three-dimensional globe translating itself into a two-dimensional map which it cannot do without undergoing significant tears and distortions.

the collapse of a higher dimensional world and from our narrow-minded perspective that can only grasp one cross section at a time, we are observing the way a multi-dimensional universe transforms into a lower dimensional state. Our earthbound minds cannot grasp its unity. Instead we observe a series of related but disconnected slices (like the orange and green of the carrot in Flatland) where each appears as an entity unto itself. We might notice that every time the orange appears the green always follows nearby. Still, there is no evidence that they evolve one from the other. Rather, they are simply, observably present.

Edenic Adam

Expelled from Eden And Descending into the Lowest World (the physical plane) and translating his ten-dimension light-body into a three-dimensional "physical body" that includes the entire evolutionary history of our universe, from the Big Bang till present time.

Triassic 225-193
Permian 280-221
Carboniferous 345-280
Devonian 395-345
Silurian 440-345
Ordovician 500-440
Cambrian 600-500

As the feet and legs of Edenic Adam collapse and translate into our three-dimensional world primitive life forms appear on the physical plane.

Cretaceous 136-65
Jurassic 193-136
Triassic 225-193
Permian 280-223
Carboniferous 345-280
Devonian 395-345
Silurian 440-345
Ordovician 500-440
Cambrian 600-500

As the torso (and vital organs) of Edenic Adam collapse down into our three-dimensional world, more complex organisms appear on the physical plane, but still not yet humans.

Quaternary 2-present
Tertiary 63-2
Cretaceous 136-65
Jurassic 193-136
Triassic 225-193
Permian 280-223
Carboniferous 345-280
Devonian 395-345
Silurian 440-345
Ordovician 500-440
Cambrian 600-500

As the head (and brains) collapse down into our world human beings first appear on the evolutionary scene.

Now, let's reread the description of Flatland, but this time from the perspective of an evolutionary biologist: the zoologist who examines the fossil records and existing family trees…

> …sees shapes [i.e. species] suddenly appear, grow and shrink, change color and then [sometimes] suddenly disappear [into extinction]. Even it he were to understand [i.e. intellectually, from the kabbala or from Superstrings] that these various objects were actually part of one higher-dimensional object, he is unable to visualize this completely, or imagine life in a higher dimensional space."[46]

Thus, what appears to be an evolutionary progression of life from simple to complex is the way that Edenic reality appears when mapped onto a four-dimensional Flatland. This means that the creatures of our world did not really originate here but actually existed as limbs and organs within the Edenic "light being" called *Adam*. The celestial *Adam* appears to us, here below, east of Eden, as a progression of discrete cross-sections, which is why the empirical evidence fits the typological model of animal classification, but does not support their continuous inter-connection as proposed by Darwin. From this perspective, the family trees of zoology are actually identifying organ

---

[46] Kaku and Trainer, 170.

systems within the primordial man. Just as a logical and visual relationship applies to the limbs and organs of a person, so on a cosmic scale were the family lines and hierarchy of species connected within *Adam*.

An evolutionary-*like* progression *was* involved in the original, multi-dimensional creation of the first six days. Yet, since the nature of physicality in Eden was different from this world, so the concept of progressive development was also different. The *midrash* teaches that God envisioned the end and perfection of the entire creative process before actually beginning the work. Then He *spoke* reality into existence, a process that took ten "statements" and seven days. Thus the evolutionary progression that applied to Genesis was a conceptual one, more akin, to thought than matter. While thought also evolves and unfolds, it is not bound by the same rules and limitations that apply to bodies. There exists, in the sphere of mind, the possibility of leaps and sudden turns, all related by a connecting theme (the stream of consciousness), but not burdened by the inertia of materiality. The evolution of mind is logical rather than physical. This is the evolutionary progression that applied to Eden, where bodies were built from thought forms instead of physical matter. This explains why, as the biologist Michael Denton puts it:

> No one has ever observed the interconnecting continuum of functional forms linking all known past and present species of life. The concept of the continuity of nature has existed in the mind of man, never in the facts of nature.[47]

Based on the new paradigm where evolution is simply an artifact of ten dimensions collapsing into three, the above statement is exactly correct. Evolutionary relationships *do* exist, but they reflect a logical progression in the realm of mind, for that is where the Bible's creation story occurred.[48]

Yet the question remains: How, literally, did the transition from ten to three dimensions occur? How did reality reconstitute itself after the fall? How did Eden don the garments of a four-dimensional world? When it collapsed and re-formulated on a lower level of reality, did it evolve according to Darwin's theory or not? The fossil evidence argues, "no." It presents a

---

[47] Michael Denton, *Evolution: A Theory in Crisis* (Burnett Books, Hutchinson Publishing Co. 1987). p. 353.

[48] As explained, the Garden of Eden was on the level of **Briyah** (i.e., the mental plane).

record of discrete and independently arising animal types. This contradicts the organic and interconnected model that Darwin proposed.

The Torah provides two possible models for answering that question. It identifies two creations in this world that are perfect and complete microcosms of the larger universe: the Tabernacle (the sanctuary built in the desert after Sinai), and the human being. Each arises in a different way, and it is not clear which is the prototype for the historical progression of life as it has occurred on this planet.

The Tabernacle's components were created independently, each from different materials, fashioned by different artisans, and then combined into a coordinated whole. This parallels the typological model of evolution. A ten-dimensional *picture*, with its pieces already intact, translates itself, slice by slice, into four dimensions. The species are not actually arising from within the four-dimensional frame itself. They are being transferred from one state to another, like a globe flattening into a map. In this model the species are related conceptually, though not ancestrally. They fit together like puzzle pieces yet arise independently through some, as yet unidentified process by which ten dimensions transfigured into four. The definitional boundaries of each species are, and have always been, discrete.

The embryological development of life illustrates the second possible mechanism of evolutionary progression. Its sequence is closer to what Darwin proposed. A soul, a higher-dimensional entity, comes down into this four-dimensional world, and proceeds through the sequence of fetal development. A single cell evolves and differentiates stage by stage, each stage evolving from the one before, and in the end becomes a single creature containing highly specialized and discrete organ systems that are as dissimilar from each other as one species from the next. All this comes about from a single cell.

Both models are consistent with Torah principles. Neither raises theological problems. Empirical evidence favors the former, yet since no scientific mechanism exists to explain it, scientists favor the latter.

Evolutionary Creationism presents a model of how science and Torah, when brought into dialogue, can solve the deepest questions of the universe in the most satisfying ways.

The Talmud declares, "God's seal is truth."[49] And since science and Torah both share a passion for truth, this becomes their holy meeting ground.

---

[49] TB Shabbat 55a; Yoma 69b; Sanhedrin 64a.

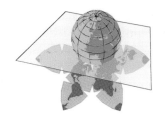

II

WHITE FIRE AND BLACK FIRE- A COSMIC ROMANCE[50]

The world-to-come is an entirely new state of reality, impossible to conceptualize, for it emerges as a discontinuous shift from everything we have known. This world "dies", its body (or coarse physical components) dissolve, and its storehouse of memories gets absorbed by the "soul."[51] The entire universe (from beginning to end) is reborn as a single radiant body of light. The *world to come* is

---

[50] The source texts for this essay appear in the Appendix as the texts numbered 9-11.

[51] For an accessible discussion of this idea in English see: R. Aryeh Kaplan, *If You Were God* (NCSY—NY, 1983) pp. 25-28).

eternal. Its distinguishing feature is freedom from suffering. The unavoidable fate of this universe-encompassing creature is to experience infinitely expanding bliss from eternally deepening intimacy with G-d.[52]

Science provides a possible mechanism for the transformation of physical reality that fulfills Judaism's vision of the *world to come*. As explained, physicists postulate a remote period of history when the cosmos had ten spatial dimensions. This early universe shattered and reorganized itself as two interconnected worlds, one with three dimensions (our own) and one with seven dimensions that collapsed into an infinite array of dense knots curled up behind each point of our time and space. These mini black holes are now invisible though scientists are busy trying to smoke them out.

> ...[Our universe] actually exists in a [11]-dimensional environment. Four dimensions of which - height, width, depth, and time - correspond to the

---

[52] Leshem, *Shaaeri Leshem*, *Zmanei HaTikun*, p. 485-520. These chapters include excerpts from R. Elyashuv's writings that develop, at length, the ideas that underlie this essay.

familiar features [of our world]. The remaining [seven] dimensions are somehow crumpled into tiny, compact balls, which correspond in physical terms to minuscule spaces only 10^{-33} centimeter wide - far smaller than a proton and effectively invisible.[53, 54]

A similar model appears in kabbala which divides the world into two types of lights called white fire and black fire.[55] These two modes of divine expression are always entwined, though sometimes only barely and sometimes to a consummate degree. They are cosmic forces that correspond to the conscious and subconscious layers of the human psyche and are then called mind-awareness and body-awareness.[56] Neither can function without the

---

[53] Science News, Vol. 43, "Strings and Mirrors" by Ivers Peterson, Feb 27, 1993 p138.

[54] Science News, Vol. 148, "Strings and Webs" by Ivers Peterson August 26, 1995 p140.

[55] TY Shekalim 25b; Zohar 3:132a. These terms, white fire and black fire, also correspond to the kabbalistic terms, *chassadim* and *gevurot*.

[56] Leshem, *HaDrush Olam HaTohu, Maamar Clali*, section 2, p2, rt (but also entire *maamar*); p. 12 rt. (1:1:2:2).

other.[57] White fire cannot impact the physical world except via the agency of its *black* counterpart which gives form and substance to its abstract concepts. Similarly, black fire, when left on its own, disintegrates into dense knots of unrealized possibility. There it waits for white fire to penetrate its shell, layer by layer, and draw forth its chaotic beauty into a stepwise sequence of actualized potential.[58]

The unification of black fire with white fire can be full or partial. The history of our universe is the saga of their joining and separating and then joining again, a cycle that recurs over and over since the beginning of time.[59] Whenever they split the universe shatters and each goes its own separate way. White fire absorbs back up to its root, while black fire collapses into cinders of dark light, called *gevurot*.

And then, as always, they begin their reapproach. The layer that we call reality is the

[57] Leshem, *HaDrush Olam HaTohu* H, Part 1, p. 91, bottom rt. (1:5:5:19).

[58] Leshem, *HaDrush Olam HaTohu*, *Maamar Clali*, section 2, p2, rt; p. 12 rt. (1:1:2:2).

[59] Ari, EC, Shaar Miut HaYareach, Chapter 2.

active seam of encounter between these two cosmic lights. As the white fire descends, it penetrates the outer surface of the *gevurot*. Like air puffs up a shrunken balloon, when touched by white fire, these dark lights spring open to unfurl a luxurious treasure of hidden beauties. From a compressed knot the size of a grasshopper antenna, their outer surface inflates to embrace the entire world. Moment by moment the white fire releases a new bundle of dark lights that expands to become our next second of time. It is this mechanism that drives the unfolding of cosmic history. [60]

And so, Jewish mysticism chronicles the odyssey of seven universes created and destroyed before our own (or 8th in the sequence.) Each was a joining of white fire with black fire that couldn't endure. This unstable phase of pre-history is called the "world of points," for its shatterings spawned myriads of these dark knots of congealed light and unactualized potential called *gevurot*.[61] These

---

[60] Leshem, *HaDrush Olam HaTohu* 2:4:18:6-8; 2:4:16:5; 2:2:3:1-4; 2:2:3:5-7.

[61] The Zohar (and subsequent kabbalistic texts) compare these *gevurot* to grasshopper antennae to convey the

cinders, strewn throughout the cosmos, became the raw materials of *our* world. We are built from the recycled debris of these seven shattered kingdoms that comprise the world of points. All the potentials of our world are packed inside their dense granules.

Like a spring squeezed tight these compressed knots of dark light are always working to release their torque. In each moment their outermost layer dissolves and expands into actualization, and in so doing it *becomes* the next moment in time and slice of cosmic history. Layer by layer these *gevurot* shed their skin releasing another part of themselves into manifest expression. It is not that they unfold *within* time, rather their unfolding actually creates the time and space and history that comprises each moment.[62]

The time sequence, then, is as follows: Before the Torah begins its chronicle of *our* world with the first verse of Genesis ("In the beginning..."), *HaShem* created and destroyed

---

idea of their minute and string-like properties. See source text #6 in Appendix.

[62] Leshem, *HaDrush Olam HaTohu* 2:4:18:6-8; 2:4:16:5; 2:2:3:1-4; 2:2:3:5-7.

seven universes in a period of history called the world of points. This building and shattering of worlds was a cosmic laboratory where Divinity forged the raw materials for our (eighth) world. The end products of this sequence are called *gevurot,* dark knots of unactualized potential, and they contain all the possibilities that can ever unfold in our universe.[63]

In the six days of creation, as told in Genesis, Divinity infused these dark knots with conscious awareness so that they unraveled to their nearly full extent. The enlightened potential locked inside each knot was released and manifest...or nearly so. And, from the midrashic descriptions of this era, we see that there were higher dimensions and scintillating lights released through their union. The multidimensional features of Eden were nothing but the cargo of these dense light granules unsprung and released into the world by the white fire of Divine consciousness. Only a small increment of their bounty was deliberately left unextricated and assigned to Adam and Chava as their life's work. In extracting the potential of this last stockpile of *gevurot* they would have

---

[63] Leshem, *Shearim V'Hakdamot*, last chapter.

become co-creators with Divinity and fulfilled their purpose in creation. Upon completing their task, the universe would have passed into the final stages of the world-to-come. Instead they sinned and all reverted back to its original, knotted state. The bulk of G-d's creation-work came undone. Light bodies regressed back into skin bodies and six dimensions collapsed into an infinite array of mini black holes (*gevurot*) that are the subfoundation of our world.

This Biblical scenario clearly parallels the sequence of events postulated by science as the origin of our universe:

> Like a dam bursting, the ten dimensional fabric of space-time ruptured violently and rapidly reformed into two [yoked and bound] universes of lower energy. Four dimensions correspond to the space-time of our world while six dimensions crumpled back down into an infinite number of dark invisible black holes that hide behind each point of space and time.[64]

---

[64] Dr. Michio Kaku and Jennifer Trainer, *Beyond Einstein: The Cosmic Quest for the Theory of the Universe* (Bantam New Age Books, 1987) p. 158.

Kabbala explains that our work in this interim period of history – from Adam's sin till messianic days – is to reintegrate these hidden lights back into our world. As explained, the *gevurot* experience a steady rate of evaporation for in each moment some increment of their dark and hidden light seeps back into our world manifesting as the concrete and abstract content of each moment, which includes, according to Kabbala, three components called: *worlds, years* and *souls*.[65]

Worlds corresponds to what science calls space with its three dimensions of length, breadth, and depth.

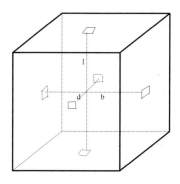

---

[65] Sefer Yetzira 3:3.

Every physical object in our world takes up space, whether it be large, small, or even microscopic. And anything that takes up space has height, breadth and depth (thickness).

l = height (length)

b = breadth (width)

d = depth (thickness)

Years corresponds to the time line of past, present, and future, which is the 4th dimension of our world. For example, to successfully arrange a rendezvous we must coordinate our meeting in four dimensions:

1 - street name = breadth (longitude)

2 - street number = depth (latitude)

3 - floor = height (altitude)

4 - day and hour = time

These first two categories which the *Sefer Yetzira* calls *worlds* and *years,* and which science calls space and time, are quite familiar. We take them for granted and don't generally think of them as formal dimensions at all. They are simply our world.

Souls. Kabbala teaches that a successful rendezvous actually requires another coordinate called *souls,* a multi-dimensional term that specifies the consciousness quotient of each participant. Every encounter is also a meeting of minds (and hearts). The axis called *souls* measures the moment's capacity for increasing consciousness.

As the *gevurot* slowly unfold into actualization and seep into our world, history evolves and consciousness expands. Evidence that their higher dimensions are infiltrating our universe appears in the realm of consciousness. As these soul lights accumulate over time they manifest as the evolution of culture, science, and consciousness.

Each dissolving layer of *gevurot* contains lights of all three sorts: *worlds, years* and *souls*. The lights from the categories of *worlds* and *years* are immediately perceptible as the time and space and events of our world. The category of *souls*, however, includes (perhaps) the extra seven dimensions that manifest as consciousness and that are also slowly but steadily seeping into the world. As the knowledge base of humanity expands through history, so does its capacity for *knowledgeable* awareness. The lights from the category of *souls* drive the expanding of consciousness that happens in the course of each life, and throughout the span of history. According to Kabbala, these missing dimensions are gradually unfurling as we come to use the full capacity of our brains.

Appendix 1

A Scientific Model That Suggests a Similar Paradigm to Evolutionary Creationism

The text that follows is a direct quote from a footnote in the *Elegant Universe* by Brian Greene, p. 411.

Some theorists see a hint of this idea in the holographic *principle,* a concept originated by Susskind and the renowned Dutch physicist Gerard 't Hooft. Just as a hologram can reproduce a three-dimensional visual image from a specially designed two-dimensional film, Susskind and 't Hooft have suggested that all of the physical happenings we encounter may actually be encoded fully through equations defined in a lower-dimensional world. Although this may sound as strange as trying to draw someone's portrait by viewing only his shadow, we can get a sense of what it means, and understand part of Susskind's and 't Hooft's motivation, by thinking about black hole entropy as discussed in Chapter 13. Recall that the entropy of a black hole is determined by the surface area of its event horizon- and not by the total volume of space that the event horizon bounds. Therefore, the disorder of a black hole, and correspondingly the information it can embody, is encoded in the two-dimensional data of surface area. It is almost as if the event horizon of the black hole acts like a hologram by capturing all the information content of the black hole's three-dimensional interior.

Susskind and 't Hooft have generalized this idea to the whole universe by suggesting that everything that occurs in the "interior" of the universe is merely a reflection of data and equations defined on a distant, bounding surface. Recently, work by the Harvard physicist Juan Maldacena, together with important subsequent work by Witten and of Princeton physicists Steven Gubser, Igor Klebanov, and Alexander Polyakov, has shown that, at least in certain cases, String Theory embodies the holographic principle. In a manner that is currently being investigated vigorously, it appears that the physics of a universe governed by String Theory has an equivalent description that involves only physics that takes place on such a bounding surface—a surface necessarily of lower dimensionality than the interior. Some string theorists have suggested that fully understanding the holographic principle and its role in string theory may well lead to the third superstring revolution.

APPENDIX 2

Another Beautiful Parallel Between Science and Torah

In a further exploration of the implications of Superstrings, Kaku and Trainer describe another feature of its multi-dimensional model of the world which accords precisely with midrashic descriptions of what will change in messianic times:

> Superstrings requires physicists to think seriously of what a higher-dimensional universe might look like…

> First of all, a ten-dimensional being looking down on our universe could see all of our internal organs, and could even perform surgery on us without cutting our skin. This idea of reaching into a solid object without breaking the outer surface seems absurd to us only because our minds are limited when considering higher dimensions

just like the minds of the Polygons on the Council. [66]

Similarly, the Midrash ascribes the following feature of messianic times:

In those days a person will no longer need the light of the sun by day nor the light of the moon by night. Rather, the opacity of the physical plane will itself radiate light, and through that a person will know that the sun has set. When the world becomes whitened a person will know that the sun has risen. A person will look at a bottle and know its contents. He will look at a pot and know what is inside. All this is because the Shekhina (Divine Feminine Presence) will be dwelling among us. [67]

---

[66] (Kaku and Trainer, Beyond Einstein, p166).

[67] Yalkut Shimoni, Isaiah 503 (תקי״ג). An interpretation of "The sun will no longer be for you a source of light." As brought in: 33# עח ד׳ אוצרות אחרית הימים.

APPENDIX 3

Summary of Core Ideas From Original Article on Evolution Published in B'Or HaTorah, 1984

The history of our material world is the story of consciousness integrating into matter. Consciousness descends, matter ascends. Evolution is the result of the downward pressing of consciousness. This drives the "earth" to produce more complex life forms that can manifest a greater range and depth of consciousness.

The more complex the organism, the more sophisticated the soul that shines through it. Each level of life is a wider angle lens that brings a new increment of consciousness into focus. Divinity alone possesses infinite consciousness, most simply defined as the range of a being's capacity to react and interact with its environment. The higher the creature, the more expressions of consciousness can manifest through it.

The Torah presents an evolutionary-like sequence of creation whereby "each day introduces a qualitatively higher level of life form."[68] "The only thing that Torah discloses about the mechanism [of this progressive development] is that it involved a partnership between God and the earth (i.e. nature)."[69]

> Both earth and the Creator collaborated to produce man. The earth brought forth his body, just as it did the bodies of all other creatures, and G-d infused him with the intellectual Soul."[70]

The implication is that whatever the "earth" did to formulate the bodies of other, creatures, so it did in the formation of man. Yet "the earth's capacity is restricted to yielding the anatomical structures . . . while it is within His God's power alone to imbue creatures with the breath of life." [71]

The human being is the last to appear in the Torah's six creation days. This makes *Adam*

---

[68] Malbim, Genesis 1:25 B.

[69] Malbim, trans. Zvi Faier, p. 125, footnote.

[70] Malbim, Genesis 1:26.

[71] Malbim, Genesis 1:25.

the outermost extremity in the unfolding of complexity. *Adam* is the axis point where creation turns and begins its upward journey back toward the Divine. "Evolution" continues, but now it assumes an inner (spiritual) expression, instead of a physical one. Until *Adam* evolution was primarily visible through the proliferation of life forms. Now, evolution is primarily visible through the proliferation of thought forms. The aim of the former is multiplicity. The aim of the latter is integration and unity. This evolution of thought forms manifests through art, science culture, etc. This is what happens when the polarities shift and consciousness now prevails over form. (See graph on following page).

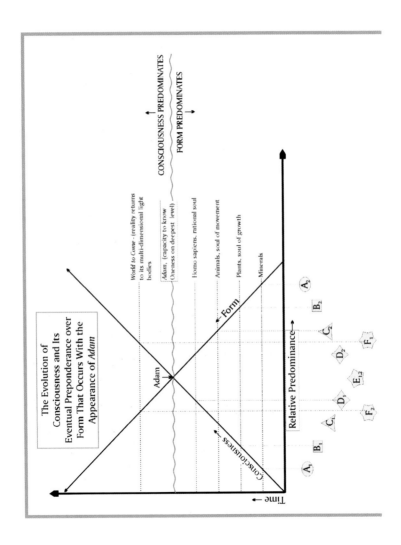

The Evolution of Consciousness and Its Eventual Preponderance over Form That Occurs With the Appearance of *Adam*

CONSCIOUSNESS PREDOMINATES

FORM PREDOMINATES

World to Come - reality returns to its multi-dimensional light bodies

Adam, (capacity to know Oneness on deepest level)

Homo sapiens, rational soul

Animals, soul of movement

Plants, soul of growth

Minerals

Form

Adam

Consciousness

Time

Relative Predominance

This table shows the relative predominance of form and consciousness at key stages in the evolution of life on this planet, starting with the mineral kingdom which appeared earliest on the evolutionary scene and so is lowest on the time scale. Its horizontal time line intersects the consciousness and form axes at points A_1 and A_2 respectively. The great distance between these two points, and the position of A_1 at the extreme left of the graph, shows that in the mineral kingdom, form prevails over consciousness to a very great degree.

The plant line intersects the consciousness and form axes at points B_1 and B_2 respectively. Since the consciousness of plants is more developed than minerals, the predominance of form over consciousness has decreased somewhat, as indicated by the shortened distance between its two intersecting points.

The animal kingdom's timeline continues this pattern. Its intersecting points, C_1 and C_2, are closer to each other still, which shows that the predominance of form over consciousness has decreased even more.

And for homo sapiens (A_1 and A_2), consciousness has developed to a point where form now only predominates to a minimal extent.

The appearance of Adam ($E_{1,2}$) marks a profoundly significant moment, where the impact of consciousness upon the external character of reality is as great as the influence of form. Adam has true free choice. He has the strength of consciousness to choose a path that differs from his instinctive reaction to the moment. (This is not always good. Sometime dismissing instincts is the right choice, sometimes it is the wrong one.)

Finally the uppermost horizontal line marks the transition between this world to the world to come. At that point in our evolutionary process form will be overwhelmed by the radiant strength of enlightened consciousness. Relative to the previous stages of evolutionary development, their relationship will invert. The form coordinate (F2) now appears further left on the graph than the consciousness coordinate, which means it will become the less predominate of the pair. The whole nature of physicality will change. Its opacity will dissolve and reality will enclothe itself in transparent bodies of light, returning to the way it was for Adam and Chava in Gan Eden before their fall.

APPENDIX 4

Kabbalistic Source Texts From Rabbi Shlomo Elyashev

1) *ספר הקדו"ש שער ו' פרקים י' וי"א)* :

ונחזור להענין כי הנה בריאת שמים וארץ וכל צבאיהם הנה היה בהאור הגנוז. וכמ"ש בבראשית רבא פ' י"ב סי' ו'. אותה האורה שנברא בה העולם. אדם הראשון עמד והביט בה מסוף העולם ועד סופו כו' עי"ש והיו עומדים עי"ז כל מעשה בראשית כולם במדרגה גבוה נעלה ונורא מאד ובפרט אדם הראשון גופה הנה הוא היה למעלה מכולם וכמ"ש בפרקי דר"א פ' י"ח ובתיקוני זוהר תיקון נ"ז ובכ"מ. אך אחר שחטא בעה"ד"ע הנה ירד הוא וכל הבריאה כולה ונתהפכו כולם מכתנות אור בא' לכתנות עור בע' שהוא משכא דחויא. כמ"ש בתרגום יונתן שם וכן בת"ז בכ"מ. והנה אז נסתלק ונתעלם כל האור דשת ימי בראשית ונתעבה ונתגשם כל הבריאה כולה ונתמעט ונתצמצם האור מאז ולהלאה ואין אנו משתמשים עתה אלא באור הפנימי המצומצם במציאת העולמות כמו שהם עתה אחר החטא. אבל הבריאה דשת ימי בראשית עצמן היה באמת רק בהאור הגנוז אלא שלא היה מתפשט האור הזה בכל מקום דהצמצום כולו כי שם נשאר מקום למדור הקליפות כנ"ל וזהו שנאמר ויבדל אלהים בין האור ובין החשך כי משום שהאור הזה הוא בלתי גבול היה צריך לעשות הבדלה ביניהם שלא יתפשט למטה ג"כ עי"י שהוא בלתי גבול והיה נשאר זה שיתוקן עי"י אדם וכנ"ל והרי לנו עכ"פ כי כל הבריאה כולו הנה היה רק בהאור דבלתי גבול אלא שע"י החטא נסתלק ונגנז :

2) *הדרוש עה"ד סימן ו' ד"ה ונחזר* :

ונחזור להענין כי הנה ע"י החטא דאדה"ר...ירדו כל העולמות כולם ונתעבו ונתגשמו ונתלבשו במשכא דחייא...

3) *ספר הדע"יה ח"ב דרוש ד' ענף י"ז* :

ובסיבת זה מיתו ונשברו ועלו גם אורות הנקודות למעלה וכמו שמתבאר כ"ז לעיל ח"א וירדו למטה רק הניצוצין עם השברי

כלים לבד ונפרדו עוד משרשן שהוא גם מאורות הנקודות ג"כ
ונעשו עי"ז לתוקף דינין קשים. והנה אותן השברי כלים הם
היו השרשים דכל העולמות ביי"ע ומציאותם אשר בכל משך
ימי עולם כולו. והניצוצין היו בחי' אצילות שבהם והרי ירדו
כל שרשי הד' עולמות אבי"ע למטה בבחי' כל חלקי הדצח"מ
שבהם שהם עולמים ונשמות. והנשמות הם היו התתקעי"מ
דורות שעליהם אמרו כי עלו במחשבה להיבראות. כמ"ש
בבראשית רבה פ' כ"ח סימן ד'. כי עולם הנקודות הוא סוד
המחשבה. שיצאו מהעי"ב דהמ"ס כאשר שעלו שם למ"ן
מלמטה מהמפרסא וכמו שבארנו לעיל ח"א. והוא סוד כוונתם
ז"ל עלו במחשבה להיבראות כי העי"ב דהמ"ס הוא סוד
המחשבה העליונא ושם עלו למ"ן ומשם יצאו דרך העינים והם
הנקודות שיצאו ומלכו ושלטו כרגע והמציאו בשליטתם את
כל השרשים דהד' עולמות אבי"ע מכל חלקי הדצח"מ שבהם
שהם עולמות ונשמות אך היו גבורות גדולות משום שהיו רק
מהמלכויות דבי"ן בהעלם אור א"ס מהם כנ"ז ועי"י תוקף
גבורתם יצאו בלי סדרים ולא היה אפשר להם להתקיים כלל
ומיתו ונשברו כליהם וירדו השברי כלים עם הניצוצין דש"כ
ופי"ר ורפ"ח למטה והם הגבורות היותר גדולים אשר גם
בהנקודות עצמן וכאשר ירדו למטה לבדן נעשו לתוקף דינין
קשים עי"י שנתנרחקו ממקורן ומאור קדושתם שלמעלה ועי"ז
הרשיעו התתקעי"מ דורות וגברו ברשעתם הרבה מאד ונעשה
מזה כל הטומאה והזוהמא והרע ובתוכה היו טבעים כל
הניצוצין והשברי כלים שהם השרשים דכל המציאיית כולם
שהיה עתיד לצאת בכל הד' עולמות אבי"ע בכל משך ימי עולם
אשר עד ביאת המשיח. והם יוצאים ומתבררים משם לאט
לאט כנ"ל בכל דברינו והם המציאיית המתחדשים בכל יום
בכל חלקי הדצח"מ כי הם מהבירורים המתבררים תמיד:

4) *חלק א' דרוש ה' סימן ה' (ד"ה 82)* :

ועי"ז נעשה ונתהווה כל מדרגות העולמות אשר למטה
מהצמצום. וכן הוא בכל עולם ועולם. כי עי"ז שאינו מאיר
העליון אלא רק דרך גוף וכלים הנה עי"ז יוצא התחתון על
מדרגתו וכן מתחתון לתחתון עד שרק עי"ז נעשה האפשרית
למציאת כל העולמות כולם עד העשיה התחתונה.

5) *חלק א' דרוש ה' סימן ז' (ד"י 83) :*

וברדתם למטה מהרגליים עמדו החיצונית דהאחור עמדו
בהמקום אשר נקרא עתה עולם הבריאה והחיצונית דהאחור
עמדו בהמקום שהוא עתה עולם היצירה ואז הוחשכו עוד
יותר וירדו החיצונית דחיצונית דהאחור יותר למטה שהוא
בהמקום הנקרא עתה עולם העשיה.

6)) *ספר הדע"ה ח"א מאמר הכללי אותיות א'-ד'*

והנה המלכים כאשר מלכו הנה היו בבחי' אורות וכלים נשמה
וגוף וכאשר מיתו עלה נשמתם למעלה והכלים ירדו למטה
ונשברו ונתפזרו לשברים אין קץ. והנה היה יירידתם במקום
העתיד להעולמות ביי"ע. אמנם כאשר ירדו השברי כלים הנה
ירדו עמהם ניצוצים רבים מהאורות ג"כ. וירדו עמהם ג' בחי'
נצוצין. א'. ש"ך נצוצין והם מהחכמה. ב'. פ"ר נצוצין והם
מהבינה. ג'. רפ"ח נצוצין והם מהדעת. כי כללות האורות הם
חב"ד וירדו נצוצין מכ"א מהם. וכמו שבארנו בדרוש ש"ך
ופ"ר ורפ"ח בשער טנת"א פי"ה. והנה אלו הנצוצין הם
מהגבורות היותר קשים ולכך נתפזרו הם לניצוצין דקים וירדו
הם למטה עם השברי כלים שהם העביות הנעשה מהדינין
תקיפין. והנה אלו הניצוצין והשברי כלים. הם השרשים
הראשונים דכל המציאיית כולם. אשר אמרנו לעיל אות א'
שנעשו במלוכת המלכים והוא בנין העולמות שהיה הקב"ה
בונה קודם התיקון דמעשה בראשית. והם היסודות
הראשונים לכל המציאות כולו וכניי"ל ומשום שהיו דינין
תקיפין מיתו ונשברו וירדו למטה ונתפזרו לניצוצין ושברים
אין קץ והוא בונה עולמות ומחריבן כנז'. אמנם אח"כ לצורך
התיקון דמעשה בראשית הנה הופיע הקב"ה את אור קדושתו
ית"ש וגילה והמשיך אור החסד ונתפשט עד למטה והעלה
ובירר מהניצוצין הנז' כל הצורך להמציאות דמעשה
בראשית. כי הרי הם השרשים הראשונים כנז'. ונתבסמו
בחסדים ונעשה מהם כל מעשה בראשית כולם. אך שאר כל
הניצוצין והשב"כ אשר היו עומדים להעשות מהם כל
המציאיית אשר בכל משך זמן דימי עולם כולו הנה הם לא עלו
ולא נתבררו עדיין כי ניתנו הם כולם להתתקן ולהתברר עי"י
מעשה אדם הראשון. ע' לקמן בח"א דרוש ו' סי' ד' אות ז'.
אמנם עי"י החטא דעהד"טע הנה לא די שלא תיקון אלא שקלקל

הרבה וכמו שיתבאר לקמן. אך עכ"פ הוא כי לא נתקנו בעת
מעשה בראשית אלא רק הצורך למע"ב אבל כל מה שהיה
עתיד לצאת בכל משך ימי עולם הם ניתנו להתתקן ע"י מעשה
התחתונים. והוא מ"ש באד"ר קל"ה ב' על התיקון דמע"ב.
מנהון אתבסמו. מנהון אתבסמו ולא אתבסמו. ומנהון לא
אתבסמו כלל. ע' מאמרי רשב"י דף מ"ד ע"ג ודף ס"ב ע"א
ובהגר"א ביהל אור פי' פקודי דף ל' ע"ב :

הנה מה שאמרנו כי במלוכת המלכים נעשו השרשים
הראשונים דכל המציאיית כולם. הנה העיקר הוא. כי מה
שנוגע להעולמות ביי"ע. הנה לא נעשה בעת מלוכתם אלא רק
בחי' אצילות שבהם. כי כל עולם הוא כלול מאביי"ע. שהם סוד
יחידה חיה נשמה רוח נפש כנודע וכמו שבארנו בספר הקדו"ש.
והנה לא נעשה בעת מלוכתם אלא רק השרשים הראשונים
אשר כך כרני חגבים מבחי' היחידה והחיה שבהם שהוא בחי'
האצילות שבהם. כי מלוכת המלכים היה בעת שהיו עומדים
כולם במקום שהיה עתיד לעולם האצילות ולכך נעשה אז
השרשים הראשונים אשר כך כרני חגבים לבחי' היחידה והחיה
דכל המציאיית כולם שהוא בחי' האצילות שבהם (ע' מאמרי
רשב"י דף כ"ב סע"ד מדפוה"ח תרנ"ח). דה"מ או יאמר ע"ש
והבן מאד) אבל השרשים הראשונים דבחי' הביי"ע שבהם
שהם החלקי דנשמה רוח נפש לכל המציאיית כולם דהעולמות
ביי"ע. הנה זה לא נעשה להם אלא רק בעת מיתתם ושבירתם.
כי מיתתם הנה היה בעת שירדו למטה ר"ל בעת ירידתם
במקום העתיד להביי"ע. והנה אז הנה יצא ונעשה מהניצוצין
והשב"כ כל השרשים הראשונים אשר כך כרני חגבים לכל
המציאיית דהביי"ע. ונעשה להם אז הבחי' דנשמה רוח נפש גוף
שבהם. שהוא בחי' הביי"ע שבהם. הנה שלא יצאו ולא נעשו אז
רק בבחי' שרשים קטנים וכקרני חגבים כנז' ונעשה כ"ז בהם
רק בעת מיתתם ושבירתם שהוא מהניצוצין והשב"כ. וזהו מה
שאמרו באד"ר קל"ה ע"ב. והא כתיב. וימת. וימת. וימת.
דאתבטלו לגמרי. לאו הכי. [ור"ל כי הרי אדרבה הוא שיצא
ונעשה מהם אז כל השרשים הראשונים דכל המציאיית כולם
דהעולמות ביי"ע] אלא כל מאן דנחית מדרגא קדמאה דהוה
ביה קארי ביה מיתה כד"א. וימת מלך מצרים כו'. כי מקודם
היו במקום העתיד לעולם האצילות ויצא אז כל השרשים
הראשונים אשר כך כרני חגבים דעולם האצילות וכן גם האצי'

דביי"ע כנזי. וזהו ענין מלוכתם. ואח"כ ירדו למטה במקום העתיד להעולמות ביי"ע ומיתו ונשברו (כי האורות יצאו מהכלים וזהו המיתה. והכלים עם הש"ך ופ"ר ורפי"ח ניצוצין ירדו למטה. ונשברו הכלים ונתפזרו השברים והניצוצין לשברים אין קץ וזהו השבירה) ואז יצאו ונעשו כל השרשים הראשונים אשר כהם כרני חגבים דכל המציאיית דביי"ע. והרי נתבאר לנו כי השרשים דהאצילות נעשה בעת מלוכתם. והשרשים דביי"ע נעשה בעת מיתתם ושבירתם. אמנם המיתה והשבירה הרי היה עכ"פ בהשרשים הראשונים דבחי' האצי' גופה כי הרי אותן שמלכו הם עצמם מיתו ונשברו וירדו למטה והם הניצוצין והשב"כ שהם השרשים הראשונים דבחי' האצי' גופה אלא שאחר שירדו יצא ונעשה מהם ג"כ השרשים הראשונים דהביי"ע אבל המיתה והשבירה והירידה הרי היה בהשרשים הראשונים דבחי' האצילות גופה :

אמנם כל מה שנעשו אז, היה רק בבחי' שרשים קטנים מאד. ונקראו בדברי האריז"ל בשם נקודות. כי לא היו רק אלא בבחי' נקודות קטנות. והם בסוד הכתוב עקודים נקודים ברודים. כי הם יצאו אחר עולם העקודים וקודם לעולם הברודים שהוא האצילות. כי הם שרשם. וכנ"ל שהם השורשים הראשונים לכל. וכנודע כ"ז בדרושי האריז"ל. ועכ"פ הוא כי לא היו אלא רק בבחי' נקודות ושורשים קטנים מאד. והנה עליהם אמרו בזוה"ק בראשית לי"ה ב'. הנטיעות כרני חגבים הוו ונהורא דלהון דקיק ולא הוו נהרין. כיון דאתנטעו ואתתקנו (והוא בעת התיקון דמעשה בראשית) אתרביאו בנהורא ואקרון ארזי לבנון. וכן הוא במדרש בראשית רבה ריש פ' ט"ו. אמר ר' חנינא כרני חגבים היו. ועקרן הקב"ה ושתלן בתוך גן עדן. והוא תיקונם אשר נתקנו אח"כ שנבררו ועלו ביסוד דהמלכות. שנקרא גן עדן. כמ"ש בשער הכוונות נ"ד ב'. ושם נתקנו בעת התיקון דמעשה בראשית כל הצורך להעולמות בריאה יצירה עשיה. והרי נתבאר לנו מכ"ז כי הענין דבונה עולמות ומחריבן לא היו לבטלה ח"ו כי אז נעשה כל השורשים הראשונים דכל המציאיית כולם וכמו שיתבאר עוד בזה למטה בעה"י בארוכה :

7) ספר הדעיה דרוש עץ הדעת סימן י"ב

וסוד הדבר מה שלא סידר המאציל ית"ש תיקון לאדה"ר ג"כ
להחזירו למעלתו הראשונה. כי הרי כן הדעת נותנת להיות זה
לעומת זה. ובכל מקום שמגיע החטא והפגם. צריך להיות
תיקון נגדו. ומה גם כי הרי מדה טובה הוא מרובה. אך סוד
הענין הוא ע"פ מה שאמרנו לעיל סימן ח'. כי האמת הוא שכל
ירידת העולמות שנעשה ע"י החטא דעהד"ע וכל המאורעות
כולם שנעשה מזה וכן כל תולדותיהם ותולדות תולדותיהם
המתיילדים מהם. בכל ימות עולם עד ימות המשיח הן בכלל
והן בפרט. הנה הם כולם מנפלאות תמים דעים קורא הדורות
מראש ובגזירת נורא עלילה על בני אדם ואין שום דבר שהוא
נגד כוונתו ית"ש חלילה וחלילה אלא הכל הוא מרצונו
והנהגתו הנעלמה ית"ש וכל מה שנעשה בסוף מעשה הוא הכל
במחשבה תחילה. כי כולם הם מהיסודות דעולם הקדות
שהוא עולם המחשבה שהיה קודם הבריאה דשתת ימי
בראשית. ועליו הוא סוד מה שאמרו מנחות כ"ט ב'. שהיתה
תשובת הקב"ה למשרבעי"ה כך עלה במחשבה לפני. ושם היה
היסוד של כל הנהגה כולה אשר מהחטא דעהד"ע עם כל
התולדות המתיילד מזה ומתחלפים ועוברים בכל תהלוכות
ההנהגה אשר עד ימות המשיח הם כולם משם. והם בסוד
בונה עולמות ומחריבן ואמר דין לא הניין לי והוא עולם התוהו
אשר שולט ועובר בכל משך ימי הגלות. וכמ"ש בתז"ח דף כ"ז
א' ב' ע"ש ובהגר"א שם. ומשום שהוא מעולם המחשבה הרי
הוא נעלם מכל כל בריה. וכן גם אחר התיקון דשתת ימי בראשית
הנה הוא ג"כ שכל מה שהוא מהבינה ולמעלה נקרא הכל
מחשבה. וכמ"ש בתיקונים קל"ב ע"ב ועי"ש בהגר"א ע"ד. ושם
הוא הרצון והגזרה על כל מה שנעשה מהפגמים כולם
והמאורעות כולם. שצריך להיות כן בדוקא. והרי אי אפשר
שישתנה וכי"ז הוא מכבשי דרחמנא ומהנהגתו הנעלמה ית"ש
שאי אפשר לעמוד עליו לשום נברא. כי כל אותה ההנהגה
הנעלמה הנה היא מה שמנהיג את הכל תמיד לתכלית תיקון
האחרון אשר עליו נאמר עין לא ראתה אלהים זולתיך. ויתגלה
תועלתם וטובם רק לעתיד כי אין השגה ותפיסה במחשבתו
שהוא זיו אורו עצמו. אמנם לעתיד תגלה וכמו שנאמר כעת
יאמר ליעקב ולישראל מה פעל אל. ויתענגו בו כל מי שהוא
בכלל הנאמר עליו וצדיק באמונתו יחיה ודי בזה:

8) *ספר הדעייה חייב חלק בי דרוש גי ענף טייז* (p. 62):

והרי נתבאר לנו מכל דברינו אשר מעניף יי עד כה גדול רוממת
מעלת ומדרגת אדהייר קודם החטא הן בהגוף שלו והן בהנרייג
שלו כי היה כולל את כל הדי עולמות אבייע ומדרגת העולמות
של אז אשר בארנום לעיל טי. והיינו כי בעת שנברא שהוא
בערב שבת קודם סוף שעה חמישית היה התחלתו אשר
ממטה למעלה מסיום הוי ראשונות דהיצירה של עתה עד
המייס דאייא דאצילות של עתה כי הרי אז היה מסיים כל
עולם העשיה בסיום הוייר דיצירה של עתה. וראש עולם
הבריאה היה מגיע אז בראש הזייא דאצילות של עתה. והנה
גופו הוא נעשה מכל הגי עולמות בייע והיה בדרך זה כי הוי
פרקים הרגליים שהם גי פרקים בכל רגל הנה הם היו מהוייית
דהעשיה שהיו אז בהוייר דהיצירה. והחלק התחתון דהגוף
אשר עד החזה היה מהדייר דהעשיה שהיו אז בהדייר
דהבריאה של עתה יאלו הדייר דהעשיה הנה הם עבר הירדן
וסוריה ומהם היה נעשה החלק התחתון הנזי דהגוף אשר
מהחזה עד הרגליים. והחלק העליון דהגוף אשר מתחת הגרון
עד החזה היה מהוייית דהיצירה שהיו אז בהוייר דהבריאה של
עתה והוא ארץ ישראל אשר שהיא בחי יצירה ומשם היה החלק
העליון דהגוף שלו אשר מתחת הגרון עד החזה. והרי נעשה כל
גופו כולו רייל הרגליים והגוף שלו אשר עד הגרון מהוייר
דהיצירה של עתה ומכל היי ספיי דהבריאה של עתה והוא
משום כהנה אז לא היה פתיחות דהעשיה שהיא מדרגת
הפתיחות דחוץ לארץ אשר עפרה טמא ואוירה טמא וכייז הוא
משום שכל העשיה כולה היא עתה נתונה ועומדת בתוך מקום
הקליפות כנייל אבל אז הרי היה סיום כל העשיה בסיום הוייר
דהיצירה שהוא למעלה לגמרי מכל מקום הקליפות שהם
בהדיית שהוא הרגלין דהיצירה של עתה ובכל היייס דהעשיה
של עתה והרי היה גם כל העשיה כולה למעלה לגמרי מכל
המקום דהקליפות ולכן לא היה אז פתיחות דהחוץ לארץ כלל
והיה אז כל העולם הזה בקדושת ארץ ישראל העיקרי שהיא
בחי יצירה וזהו מה שהיו הוייית דהעשיה בהוייר דיצירה והוא
מה שהיה כל חוייל בקדושת אייי העיקרי. והדייר דהעשיה
שהם עבר הירדן וסוריא שהם כאייי ואינם כאייי לגמרי הנה
הם היו אז בקדושת ירושלים לגמרי ולכן אמרו רזייל עתידה
ירושלים שהתתרחב עד דמשק והוא משום שכן היה בעת

בריאת אדם הראשון...והגרון שלו הנה היה נעשה מהד״ר
דהיצירה שהיו אז במדרגת הנוק׳ דאצילות...וכל זה היה בעת
שנברא אמנם מסוף שעה חמישית דערב שבת בראשית
שנתעלו אז כל העולמות כולם והיה סוף העשיה בסיום הו״ר
דהבראה וראש עולם הבריאה היה מגיע בראש האימא
דאצילות של עתה...כי גופו והנרנח״יי דבי״ע היה מגיע עד
הראש האימא דהאצילות של עתה והנר״ן דהאצילות שבו
היה מגיע עד הרישא תנייינא דא״א שהוא במדרגת הנשמה
לנשמה והרוח שבו היה מהמ״ס של עתה שהוא מדרגת
היחידה כי היתה מבחי׳ אור דנפק מאויר שהוא האור הגנוז
שאדם מסתכל בו מסוף העולם עד סופו. והרי לנו גוגל
רוממות מעלת אדה״ר קודם החטא :

אמנם אחר שנכשל וחטא בעהד״ע הנה ירדו כל העולמות
כולם...למדרגת שהם עתה...כי כל הנר״ן שהיה לו מאצילות
עלו למעלה וכל עלו ונסתלקו ממנו ג״כ...הזיהרא עלאה אשר
עלה למעלה ונסתלק ממנו...וכן נאבד ממנו ג״כ כל אורות
דנרנח״יי אשר בכל הט׳ ספי׳ התחתונים...הנה הם כום נאבד
ממנו אך הם לא עלו למעלה אלא שהם ירדו ונפלו בתוך
הקליפות ומהם הוא כל הנשמות בני אדם עד ביאת המשיח...

GLOSSARY

Adam and *Chava* (Adam and Eve) – The archetypal man and woman in the Bible's creation story. The original human being was created as a single body combining both male and female aspects who were, together, called *Adam*. Only later were these two halves separated into a man and woman. The souls of all humanity derive from this archetypal human being.

Asiyah – The lowest of the four planes of existence (physical, emotional, mental, spiritual). It is the realm where light has assumed a material form. *Asiyah* means literally, the World of Action.

Atzilut – The highest of the four planes of existence (physical, emotional, mental, spiritual). It is the realm of pure archetypes and means literally, the World of Emanation.

Bible – There are twenty-four books in the Jewish Bible (called *Tanakh*). They include the Torah (5), the Prophets (8), and the Writings (11).

Briyah – The second highest of the four planes of existence (physical, emotional, mental, spiritual). It is the mental plane and means literally, the World of Creation, in part because creation (i.e., Genesis) occurred there.

Chassadim / chesed lights (generosities) – Lights of conscious awareness. The *chassadim*, when integrated, always inspire a generosity of spirit.

Dimension – One of the independent coordinates required to specify uniquely a point in space-time. For example, to arrange a successful appointment one must specify four coordinates: street name (length), street number (the perpendicular, or width), floor number (height), and time of meeting.

Evil – Literally, broken or unstable. The illusion of existence as separate and independent from God.

Gevurot – A term which means, literally, severities, and refer to the dark knots of unrectified potential that are the driving force behind our universe. *Gevurot* are generally associated with unconscious lights and with the feminine. They originated in the World of Points

God – A simple, working definition is derived from the four-letter, essential name of God, which is built from all the permutations of the verb, "to be." It thus translates as, *that which was, is, and will always be.* God is beyond gender, containing both male and female elements as well as levels of oneness where even the duality of gender does not exist.

Kabbala – Literally, the received tradition *or* the science of correspondences. That part of the Jewish oral tradition which presents the inner and mystical interpretations of the Torah and its practices. It corresponds to the S of PaRDeS.

Lights – *Lights* are always equivalent to consciousness in kabbalistic writings.

Messianic Era – A transitional time between *this* world and the next. It begins somewhere towards the end of the sixth millennium (we are now within the period of its likely beginnings) and will take us to the threshold of the world-to-come. It is the joyous stage of actualized perfection. Love of G-d, love of neighbor, and love of Torah reign.

Midrash, *midrashim* (pl) - That part of the Jewish oral tradition that explains the Biblical text through the use of stories and sermons. The *Midrash* often fills out a sparsely written Biblical narrative providing background, context, moral lessons, or legal implications. *Midrash* corresponds to the D of PaRDeS.

Names of God – The No-Thing that is all things, defies name and adjective. Nevertheless Divinity also expresses itself through an infinite variety of attributes. Judaism ascribes different names to these various modes of Divine expression. For example *Havaya* (pronounced *A-donoi*) refers to God's transcendence and *E-lohim* refers to the aspect of God that manifests as nature and natural law.

Oral Law or Oral Tradition – The explanations and elaborations of the written law or Torah. These were also received by Moses at Sinai, but passed from mouth to ear, teacher to student, until just after the destruction of the Second Temple. The first recording of the oral law was the *Mishna* (180 CE), and this opened the way for all subsequent transcriptions of what ideally was to be a personal, verbal transmission of knowledge and information. Included in the category of the oral tradition are the *Mishna, Midrash, Gemara,* Talmud and *Kabbalah.* These are still aspects of the oral tradition, even though they are written down. All Jewish teachings besides the Bible itself are considered part of the oral tradition.

PaRDeS – Literally, "orchard." Acronym for the four levels of Torah study: *pshat* (plain, literal meaning of the text); r*emez* (hints and allusions in the text); *drash* (additional levels of meaning derived by verbal analogy); and *sod* (the esoteric, mystical dimension of the text).

Sefira, Sefirot (pl) - The ten channels of Divine flow and emanation which link the Transcendent Light with Its evolving and apparently finite creation.

Shabbat – Sabbath. The seventh day of the week from Friday sunset to Saturday dusk. It is a day of rest from labor and business activity. The year 6000 in the Jewish calendar begins the 7th millennium or Sabbath of Creation (we are now in the year 5765).

Shekhina - The feminine expression of G-d, wherein is concentrated all the Divine light that shines to the lower worlds.

Shema – Literally, "Hear [Know]." The central declaration of Jewish faith which reads, in English, "Hear (Know) Israel, *God* is our Lord, God is One."

Soul – The spiritual essence of a person or thing, its life force and consciousness. To a certain degree a creature's soul is made apparent by its capacity to respond and interact with its environment, and so to manifest a particular range of the infinite continuum of potentialities that exist within Divine consciousness.

String Theory (also Superstrings) – A unified theory of the universe postulating that the fundamental ingredients of nature are not particles but tiny one-dimensional filaments called strings.

Talmud – The main repository of the Jewish oral tradition scribed in 499 CE, that interprets and elaborates the Torah.

Tetragrammaton – It refers to the four-letter, unutterable name of God which emphasizes the transcendent, eternal, and compassionate attributes of Divinity. It is pronounced *Adon-oi* when encountered in prayer and study.

Torah - The first five books of the Bible revealed at Sinai. The word "Torah" often is used to refer to both the written and oral teachings and then denotes the entire body of knowledge generated since Sinai by the Jewish people throughout history.

Tree of Knowledge of Good and Evil – The forbidden tree in Eden that represents a fallen state of consciousness where truth is twisted by emotional attachments and narcissistic filters.

World To Come – The seventh millennium and period following the messianic era that marks an entirely new state of existence where physicality, as we know it, dissolves and creation returns to its multi-dimensional, light-filled Eden.

Worlds – refers both to the four planes of reality (physical, emotional, mental, spiritual) and to the sequential stages in creation's unfolding.

APPLICATION FORM
to A Still Small Voice

Name_____

Date _____ Date of Birth _____

Address_____

_____

Tel._____Fax_____

Email_____

Profession_____

Education_____

Please enclose a $15.00 enrollment fee plus tuition:
Israel: $60/quarter (3 mos.) or $210/year
Abroad: $75/quarter (3 mos.) or $260/year
20% discount/person for groups of 5 or more

Payment is valid in foreign currency according to the US$ equivalent.

Mail application or request for more information to:

A Still Small Voice
P.O.B. 14503
Jerusalem 91141
ISRAEL
See copyright page for the telephone, fax, email,
and website of **A Still Small Voice**.

A STILL SMALL VOICE is a correspondence school that presents classic Judaism as a powerful path of spiritual transformation. Its weekly lessons draw from all aspects of the Jewish religious tradition; from its most hidden and kabbalistic mysteries to its most basic principles of faith and practice. A year and a half of weekly lessons are currently available:

Prayer and Destiny explores the mystery of prayer and how it is a potent tool for personal and spiritual growth (even more effective than visualization and affirmation). **20 weeks**.

The Enlightened Body shows how the system of Jewish ritual practices is actually a powerful and penetrating spiritual path. **12 weeks**.

Synchrony is an experiential exploration of the six constant *mitzvot*. Among the 613 religious obligations that comprise the Jewish path, six are meditations that one must hold in mind at all times. **13 weeks**.

Time Trekking explores the deeper meanings behind the daily, weekly, monthly and yearly cycles of observance. **26 weeks**.

ENROLLMENT BENEFITS INCLUDE:

weekly lessons of stimulating and practical insights into Jewish wisdom.

personal guidance through practical exercises that aid integration of the material.

timely holiday supplements.

answers to personal questions about lessons, and other topics of Jewish thought.

time tested tools guaranteed to enhance peace of mind and quality life.

The Golden Thread

שירת המינים

The Golden Thread is a homeopathically produced
remedy based on Kabbala. It is designed to heal
the deepest level of soul that was
damaged by our collective partaking of
The Tree of Knowledge of Good and Evil.

The Golden Thread

Produced in Israel by
A Still Small Voice
www.thegoldenthread.org

A STILL SMALL VOICE

PRESENTS THE FOLLOWING RESOURCES:

CORRESPONDENCE SCHOOL: A STILL SMALL VOICE is a correspondence school that presents classic Judaism as a powerful path of spiritual transformation. Its weekly lessons draw from all aspects of the Jewish religious tradition; from its most hidden and kabbalistic mysteries to its most basic principles of faith and practice. A year and a half of weekly lessons are currently available: The course titles are: Prayer and Destiny (20 weeks.); The Enlightened Body (12 weeks); Synchrony (13 weeks.); Time Trekking (26 weeks.).

HOMEOPATHIC REMEDY: THE GOLDEN THREAD is a homeopathically produced remedy based on Kabbalah. It is designed to heal the deepest level of soul that was damaged by our collective participation with the Tree of Knowledge of Good and Evil.

A Kabbalistic
Healing Remedy

KABBALISTIC WRITINGS ON THE NATURE OF MASCULINE AND FEMININE: This book presents a vision of how man and woman will relate when they have healed themselves and fixed the world. Based on a Talmudic tale about the sun and moon; Jewish mystical writings identify seven stages of waning and waxing that mark the feminine life cycle. In the final stage, *woman* stands equal and opposite to *man* and they meet for the first time as spiritual, intellectual and emotional mates. This perfect marriage has been our yearning for six thousand years, and from its consummation flow all promised blessings of the world to come.

A STILL SMALL VOICE

P.O.B. 14503, Jerusalem, 91141 Israel • tel/fax: (02) 628-2988
smlvoice@netvision.net.il • www.amyisrael.co.il/smallvoice/

PVRIM BVRSTS: This book uses the holiday of Purim to segue into the deepest kabbalistic mysteries. For example, an excerpt: "This day is called *Purim* because its inner service *is* lots. ... One goes deeply inward (and upward) to find a place inside that transcends craving and aversion. Ones love-bond to God gets so deep, one's vision  so vast, that the truest (and normally hidden) truth becomes real: Every moment is an opportunity for closeness with God and it is not clear which builds intimacy more, the joy or the pain, the blessing or the curse, Mordechai (the hero) or Haman (the villain). Would there be Purim without Haman? Who do we thank more for this day?"

EATING AS TIKVN: This book notes that humanities first error was an act of unholy eating (from the Tree of Knowledge), which means that only its opposite can fix it. All of life and all of history are training us for one end: to learn to "eat" in holiness, to not let the world's pleasures wrench our attention from G-d (even for an instant).

MEDITATION AND LEARNING RETREATS IN JERVSALEM: The goal of these retreats is to create an atmosphere that enables people to access the full healing, guiding, and enlightening potential inherent on Shabbat. There is a wealth of "light" and bounty that comes into the world with Shabbat but for most people this remains an untapped resource. One sure way to harness its potential for healing and transformation is through the practice of retreat.

TAPE SERIES
—Mystical Months
—Prayer and Destiny
—Chassidic Topics

PRIVATE COUNSELING: In addition to her writing and classroom teaching, Sarah Yehudit spends a significant amount of her time in private teaching and counseling.

About The Author

Sarah Yehudit (Susan) Schneider is the founding director of A Still Small Voice, a correspondence school that provides weekly teachings in classic Jewish wisdom to subscribers around the world. Sarah is the author of *Kabbalistic Writings on the Nature of Masculine and Feminine,* published by Jason Aronson, Inc., in 2000, (available at www.amyisrael.co.il/smallvoice/). In addition, she is the author of *Eating as Tikun* and *Purim Bursts,* as well as numerous essays published in a variety of journals and anthologies. Sarah Yehudit has a BA in Molecular, Cellular, and Developmental Biology from the University of Colorado in Boulder. Since 1981, she has lived in Jerusalem, followed an orthodox path of observance, and immersed herself in the study of mystical texts. In addition she completed the program for advanced study at Neve Yerushalayim Seminary for Women. Sarah Yehudit teaches a variety of weekly classes in Jerusalem as well as offering private instruction to individuals seeking a more personal encounter with text.

And God
said, "Go out,
and stand upon the
mountain before My
Eternal Presence..." and a
great and strong wind rent the
mountains and broke the rocks in
pieces...but the Presence was not in the
wind. And after the wind an earthquake,
but the Presence was not in the earthquake.
And after the earthquake a fire, but the
Presence was not in the fire. And after the
fire a still small voice. And when Elijah
heard it he wrapped his face in his mantle
and went out and stood in
the entrance of the
cave.

(I Kings 19:11 13)